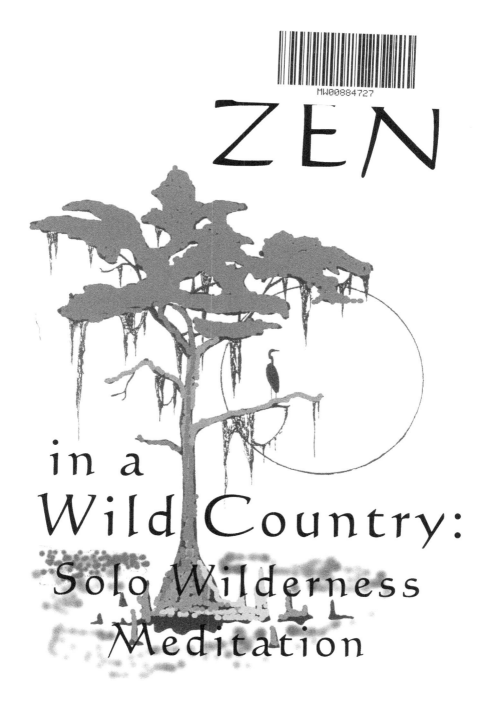

ZEN

in a
Wild Country:
Solo Wilderness
Meditation

ANNE RUDLOE

"One merges into another…until the time when what we know as life meets and enters what we think of as non-life: barnacle and rock, rock and earth, earth and tree, tree and rain and air. And the units nestle into the whole and are inseparable from it. Then one can come back to the microscope and the tide pool and the aquarium. But the little animals are found to be changed, no longer set apart and alone. … man is related to the whole thing, related inextricably to all reality, known and unknowable. …. all things are one thing and that one thing is all things – plankton, shimmering phosphorescence on the sea and the spinning planets and an expanding universe…. It is advisable to look from the tide pool to the stars and then back to the tide pool again."

John Steinbeck,
Log from the Sea of Cortez

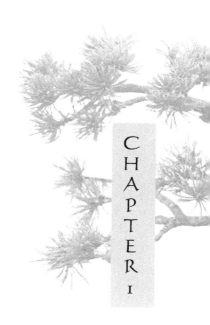

CHAPTER 1

THE SWAMP

Whoever says, "Without having attained
concentration, I will go live in solitude, in
an isolated wilderness place, " it can be
expected that that one will either sink to
the bottom or float away on the surface.

Anguttara Nikaya 10:99 (Buddhist Sutta)

Bushes slapped hard against the windows and clean whitewall tires of a shiny rental car as it splashed through puddles on a rutted dirt road south of Tallahassee. Uncle Charles had just arrived from New York for a visit and my husband and I wanted him to see our swamp — a little island of private land in the middle of a federal wildlife refuge that we had bought years earlier. After lurching over a washed-out section and getting past the place where the big car was in danger of getting stuck, we arrived at the edge of Alligator Lake. Sunlight flashed on the black water. We got out and stood gazing at twisted cypress roots and the spot where wild hogs had grubbed up the leaf litter.

"This is it?!" Uncle Charles finally stammered.

"Sure is," Jack said proudly.

There was a long pause as we all stared out over the cypress trees and black water.

"You're crazy!" Uncle Charles finally said slowly and emphatically. "Why, why, it's nothing but a swamp!"

He said swamp with loathing, as if great scaly things with teeth and slime were going to reach up any minute to pull us all down into the abyss.

"Why?" he asked incredulously. "You could have bought a waterfront lot or a business site, some investment land down here. But this…!"

The answer was difficult to put into words. It was the classic case of selling Florida swamps to suckers, but unlike most suckers, we knew what we were doing. In order to exist on that pastoral Gulf Coast shoreline with its quiet bays, salt marshes and unspoiled woodlands, we led the frenetic existence of free-lance professionals. Marine biologists and writers, we ran a tiny nonprofit aquarium in north Florida and wrote books about the ocean. I taught ecology and marine biology part time at a local university. A precarious life, it was dependent upon the unforgiving sea for survival, both financially and sometimes literally. For us, the swamp was a place to escape for a few hours and clean out our souls. And we had bought a refuge from the carscape that was overwhelming much of the rest of the area.

The next day, after our still appalled relative left, we went back with a canoe and our two sons. We wanted to look at it again through different eyes. As we paddled into the lake, the lily pads boiled and we came face to face with the largest alligator we'd ever seen, every bit as big as the canoe. As frightened as we were, it surged ahead, running away from us and throwing a wake. In the distance, wood ducks rose and noisily winged their way across the lake.

"Look!" screamed our younger son Cypress, jumping up and pointing at the gator.

"Sit down!" Jack and I shouted together as the canoe lurched over. Sky threw himself the opposite direction and we all somehow stayed afloat.

"Don't you ever do that! I thought you were old enough to know better or you wouldn't have come," snapped Jack.

"OK, OK, not to worry," Cypress said defiantly but he sat rigid for the rest of the trip across the lake. Veering away from our reptilian escort, we beached our canoe between two buttressed cypresses and slogged our way up onto a high ridge. It was strange to think we owned this. Before, we could go to this forgotten swampland only because no one bothered to stop us. Now, we had guaranteed access and the knowledge that it would not suddenly be bulldozed. That meant something even though during summer, no one but the chiggers, biting flies, mosquitoes and ticks owned it.

Beyond the dark, canopied cypress forest was an open expanse of sunny lily pads and lotus flowers. In the morning mists, the cypresses and cabbage palms formed eerie shapes. The forests and swamps were alive with deer, turkey and bears. Bald eagles nested along the coastal marshes a few miles away. The lake shore swarmed with millions of tadpoles in the spring and further out, the deeper parts of the lake were full of brim, crappie and the large-mouthed bass that lurked in ambush under the lily pads. Scaly grey fence lizards with bright blue tails darted under the scrub oaks.

We knew the swamp really wasn't ours. All the property deeds and records in the courthouse were meaningless to the lily pads and cypress trees, the sunlight filtering through massive oaks, the resurrection ferns gleaming with water droplets after a rain. We could alter the land, change it, even destroy it entirely. Or we could do our best to protect it during our lifetime — but we could never own it. No one could.

I used the land as a place to camp on forest meditation retreats. Years before, I had begun practicing Zen meditation in order to better handle the mental challenges of each day, and it had eventually become a major focus of this intense and always uncertain way of life. For years, whenever daily life got too intense, I had trusted the sea and the forest to put personal issues into a larger more serene perspective.

A retreat is an exploration, a venture step by step into unknown aspects of mind, moment by moment, breath by breath. When the daily routine disappears, whether we are in a forest, a monastery or on a long solitary trip, we sometimes don't know what we are anymore and we begin to ask, "What am I doing?" From "What am I doing?" it's a very short jump to "What am I?" Seemingly doing nothing, we watch the mind, noticing the flux of thoughts and emotions that endlessly arise and dissolve, observing our minds the way a scientist observes an ecosystem. Stepping out of the routine daily environment increases the probability that the mind might step outside of its routine ways of perceiving the world and then be able to perceive in a different way. The thinking mind may eventually slow down.

The mind is strongly influenced by the environment in which it is operating, and in routine daily living, it tends to stay focused on business and family, personal achievement and status. We define ourselves by what we do and those affairs intrude incessantly into efforts to focus on spiritual issues over a brief period of time. Daily life is complex and frenetic so sitting down to meditate for a little while in the midst of everything else usually means that we take all our daily concerns into the sitting. It is very difficult to get past the total identification with personal ego based reality when practicing meditation at home. Even in a weekend or one-week retreat, most people stay focused on solving personal issues that are draining energy day-to-day, especially struggling with why anger or sadness keep arising. Even if we force the mind to be still for a little while, all the problems are just waiting unchanged when we resume thinking. It usually takes a long time for some space to arise between awareness of this moment and all our daily life concerns.

Since the forest, the desert and the ocean are nonverbal and vastly transcend human ego, they are ideal settings for this search in places where the climate is warm enough to allow practicing outdoors. Valid insights are more easily found in a wilderness/nonhuman setting where the demands and desires of the ego cannot change anything. The natural world endlessly presents its truth until we finally notice it and perhaps someday comprehend something.

A forest is always more vast and subtle than any personal issues, a good place to experience the ways in which the planet is alive, sentient, communicative and creative. The famous 19th century naturalist John Muir said, "Only by going alone in silence, without baggage, can one truly get into the heart of wilderness." One could equally well say "By going alone into the wilderness, without baggage, one can truly get into the heart of silence."

As an ecologist, I had spent years studying and teaching Florida ecosystems at a local university, but the difference between the study of ecosystems and being immersed in one was amazing. Studying ecosystems gave no clue to how alive and alert and aware and busy it was. Peering out through windows didn't come close to living in it. I was surrounded by other living beings everywhere - palmettos and trees, birds and insects and oak toads.

Hearing is a better sense than sight in the forest. I recognized animals by the sound they made even though I usually never saw them. An invisible snake rustled through the palmettos at the edge of the field. The chorus of bird song, the roaring and tail-slapping of an alligator in the lake, the raucous gabbling of a pair of barred owls, a deer splashing around in the water behind the tent all kept the place in an uproar. At night, an army of frogs roared in the darkness. By day butterflies, dragonflies, and hummingbirds darted, accompanied by an endless droning of carpenter bees in a dead tree. The birds, insects and plants created an alive conscious space that was utterly different from a building of lifeless walls and artificial lights. Being indoors cuts us off from the very thing that we are seeking, perception of the sentient energy of the universe and the experience of being a part of it. Walls, floors, ceilings, glass and electricity and the lack of natural sounds can be mental prison walls.

A formal temple-based meditation retreat uses sleep deprivation and the physical struggle to sit motionless for long periods of time as tools to still the mind. Out in the forest, with a plastic chair and the ability to wiggle a little, the body naturally became more still than in struggling to remain rigidly motionless on a cushion in a group setting. Practicing meditation in a temple had always been a physical struggle for me but in the forest it was purely a gift I was giving myself.

In the forest, mind automatically settles and becomes still, as it does while gazing at water or staring into a fire. Sitting in the gorgeous late afternoon light with all the colors at their most intense, it felt like home, as if I were accessing the Pleistocene reality in which humans all once lived. It was part of the casual beauty that is all around us if we simply stop to notice, a parallel universe a millimeter away. In the mornings, sunlight glittered on the water within a tunnel of trees and gilded the pine needles overhead. Blue sky, cool breeze, bright gold sun, orange fritillary butterflies pouring through, I had barely noticed them before as I rushed through the business of daily life.

Going to the wilderness to meditate is among the oldest of spiritual techniques. Jesus spent 40 days alone in the desert. Many early Christians, known as the Desert Fathers, followed his example. Almost 500 years earlier, when the Buddha left his royal life to seek Truth, he went to the forest and Buddhists monastics have followed that example ever since. Ancient Buddhist texts direct us to "the forest, the root of a tree, a mountain, a ravine, a hillside cave, a jungle thicket, an open space" as the best place to practice meditation. Chinese Zen kong ans (koans) show monks continuing the tradition of wandering in the wilderness centuries later.

Wilderness practice is not just to avoid the busywork of home and office – there is something unique to be found there. According to Thanissaro Bhikku, a contemporary American monk who teaches in the forest tradition,

"Wilderness plays three roles in early Buddhist texts: a place, a mode of livelihood, and an attitude toward practice. First, the wilderness is a place whose solitude, dangers, and rugged beauty provide an ideal environment for practice. The Buddha himself is said to have gained bo-dhi (awakening) in the wilderness and to have encouraged his disciples to practice there as well. ...monks and nuns were enjoined to cultivate wilderness as an attitude, an inner solitude and non-complacency tran-scending all external environments." Until the forests were cleared, forest wandering monks practiced in rural Thailand into the mid-20th century as they did during the time of the Buddha. The forest monks believed that a life in wild country led to self-knowledge.

In December the local forest was wood ducks in the cypress trees. In April it was frogs, birdsong, lightning bugs, and wildflowers, ponds ablaze with submerged yellow bladderwort flowers. When the sparkle-berry and titi were in bloom white flowers shone everywhere against green leaves, red coral bean flowers attracted hummingbirds, candles of new magnolia leaves shone in the moonlight. Dawn and sunrise, mid-morning sun on the tall pines, noonday light and blazing white heat, the intense saturated color of late afternoon, the last pale yellow glimmer of light with black tree silhouettes after sunset, uncountable small white stars in branches by night, these would be my companions.

Driving to the campsite where I would stay for several weeks felt like the beginning of a bigger newer adventure than anything that could begin with getting on a plane. While I had traveled to temples for Zen meditation retreats for many years, it was now time to integrate Zen practice into the world of forest and sea in which I actually lived. Al-though called Alligator Lake on the map, most of the land was really a wet prairie full of pond lilies and marshes with an expanse of open water on one end. Cypress and black gum trees fringed the basin with red maples and water-loving slash pines in areas that flooded in rainy months. The majestic huge pines stood on open needle-covered ground because the occasional standing water kept undergrowth from surviv-ing. The slanting intense light of early morning and late afternoon cre-ated a cathedral-like effect. The tent was nestled in palmettos within a grove of big water oaks.

Sitting, walking, sitting, walking the next morning as the sun rose on the first day of the retreat. Inside the black gum swamp around the lake shore, robins darted about feeding on red titi berries. The woods were solid birdsong punctuated by a few woodpeckers hunting insects. Sud-denly there was a loud KHU! KHU! KHU! KHU! KHU! and something big and scared crashed off in the bushes. It was a deer, a wild pig or a bear. A panther wouldn't make all that racket. Most likely it was a deer that was frightened by my presence but it could have been a deer being attacked by something, I worried. Maybe I should have sat with my back against a tree. Maybe I should have sat on the downwind side of the tree since a predator would probably approach from that direction. According to official records of the local wildlife agencies there were no panthers in the region but I knew one had been hanging around a fisherman's house on the refuge boundary five miles away attracted by the smell of old crab traps and I had seen a panther only a few miles from here.

And come to think of it, my mind continued tensely, two cypress trees in the pond by the camp had their bark shredded by a bear. On the way back to the tent, I found the deer browsing down in the cypresses along the lake shore, unconcerned with my imaginary panthers. In the five-acre field a flock of hundreds of boat-tailed grackles had settled into three trees chirping and calling in a huge racket. Then a sudden silence settled and they all flew, circled around to some other trees, settled in and started the chorus again. They repeated the sequence three times until they found the right trees and stayed there chirping for thirty minutes. Only the birds knew why those particular trees were the right ones. Life swarmed on the planet's surface, including the bit of conscious awareness labeled Anne.

The sound of the wind in the trees became the flow of time, the voice of reality moving like a river. It's always there, always flowing, usually unnoticed beneath the clutter of commitments and schedules but always there. Sometimes we clear away the mental clutter and notice. In July, the low ground cover of runner oak and wire grass added a layer of bracken fern fronds floating above the grass. The turkey oak and pine trunks passed through it all, up to the sky. The forest is always talking, always noisy, but in the hot summer its voice came as crickets and humming flying insects. The wind died leaving only hot sun pouring down in a flood. And insects. Insects flying, crawling, hustling urgently around and over and under and past the ferns and oaks that sat motionless in the sun. Here were two opposite approaches to life: plants sat quietly gathering the sunlight while the insects hustled and buzzed. Except for the ubiquitous gnats and ants, almost every large insect that flew by was a different species. A small grasshopper, bright green with a broad black stripe down its back and a thin white pinstripe on each side explored my hand for a minute. It had sky blue eyes and antennae 10 times as long as its body. When it bit, I sent it on its way, no wiser than I was.

Do the flying insects in their endless diversity divide up the various elevations above the ground? Do they have different preferred flying heights? When I stood or walked the ruthless biting flies (who have no compassion, that's not their reality) attacked, but when I sat they left me in peace. Insects were the abundant obvious owners of the place at ground level but there was a subdued quiet background of birdsong as well. Birds and insects and plants are what a forest is about. The odd snake or mammal is only an exclamation point. Those who come looking only for big things and declare the forest empty and boring miss the point.

Forest practice meant freedom to sit and walk as I needed, freedom to find the best balance of contemplative practice and action. Over the first few days, a schedule arose spontaneously. With no clock to time anything, dawn, dark and midday were the only time markers. Wake at dawn, chant and sit until sunrise, then do a long walking meditation around the field. Prostrations and yoga, then personal clean-up, morning chanting, sitting and walking in the forest using plastic chairs because of the damp ground, eat breakfast, an hour or so of manual work each day clearing underbrush, then a longer sitting around the forest. A midday break and lunch came when the sun was directly overhead. Easy to time on a clear day, it had to be guessed at on a cloudy day. Then more chanting, walking and sitting until the sun was at tree top level. Evening chanting came around sunset, then sitting in the tent until dark, more prostrations and yoga.

The formal Zen practice methods like washing bowls and drinking the rinse water, walking meditation, removing shoes at an entrance seem like rituals in a Zen center, but here they were simply practical ways to do things. Walking meditation became walking mindfully from place to place instead of endlessly walking in circles inside a room. The tradition that monks and nuns don't eat after noon made perfect sense in a forest where the logistics of meals is difficult and time-consuming. Eating only once a day left a big block of the rest of the day and night for uninterrupted meditation. The traditional precept against storing food was wise because storing fresh or cooked food in the heat could result in food poisoning. Since I couldn't go to supportive neighbors on a daily alms begging round like traditional monks, I had brought dried rice and beans and fruit.

Sit silently for a while without talking to yourself and creative insights may suddenly arise like a silvery fish suddenly darting in front of you. Sit still even longer and the silver insight fish may themselves disappear. Then another possibility arises. At the core of all major religions are experiences that are profound, vast and Real. Even though these altered mental states are more real than familiar analytical verbal thought, they are rarely experienced because they require a letting go of speech and of our habitual ego-based verbal thinking state of mind, something that seems almost impossible but is the point of meditation.

Though the experience can happen spontaneously for a few rare individuals, it more generally requires a full time monastic level effort and even then, it may or may not happen. Since the experience is rare and transient, most people never experience it and then dismiss it as unreal or imaginary, denying that it even exists. More often, we fill in the gaps with what we imagine and what we want to be the case. That process gives rise to all the various theologies and philosophies. Intellectual theories of metaphysics and theology become beliefs. We then cling to, depend on and eventually fight over those beliefs. All of this greatly weakens the mind of inquiry which could otherwise lead to the experience of Reality. The work of mystics in all religious traditions is to directly experience the reality of these alternate mental states, using techniques such as silence, intensive meditation or prayer.

While the wordless states may pop up more frequently with more continuous retreat meditation, most of our time is spent not in some nonverbal wordless altered mental state but within the thinking verbal mental state. Verbal rational teachings such as the philosophical arguments in Buddhist sutras (texts) can be helpful to keep practice in mind in daily life in between retreats. Chinul and Sosan Taesa, two of the greatest teachers in the Korean Zen tradition, both recommended the integration of rational study and meditation. The contemporary teacher Seung Sahn said that with enough silent practice, we will know how to better use words and speech. Reading books about Zen with a normal daily life state of mind is of limited use, however. Zen texts, in particular, are famously paradoxical. Most people will not experience the mental states the writers are trying to communicate without extended silent non-verbal solitude. Cultivate silence in a retreat and then the written text becomes clearer.

Time spent in this way is the unfolding of a creative process. The longer the retreat, the more it unfolds. But then life goes on, the newly formed habits from the training fade and the old mental habits re-emerge, so we periodically go back and retrain – and each time, whether in a temple or in the forest, we have more experience of how to do this consistently and effectively.

There are several very broad stages to practice. The first is attraction, intrigue, and a good dose of confusion. Then comes reading and conceptual understanding as well as examining one's personal life story and seeing the accuracy of the teachings within one's life, a phase that often takes years. Eventually one begins to relax enough to let go of conceptual thought, become still and see what arises out of that stillness. One teacher commented "Relying only on analytical intelligence and memory limits the possibilities. Instead just act completely with no idea of whether it is will be right or wrong, continually look into the question, 'am I obscuring my clarity just now?' and then surprise is possible."

Practice doing this enough and from this other mental states may arise – sometimes joy, and equanimity, sometimes non local mental events and sometimes perception of Reality beyond name and form. It may become possible to function out of this awareness in daily life, moment to moment with clear still mind unless talking and thinking is needed. Formal intense meditation practice alters the brain in the direction of directly perceiving what is normally beyond the limits of brain based, ego dominated mind. It also helps to optimize living this life here and now in this body in a wiser way.

During the morning sutra-chanting sessions at my forest campsite, I kept the rhythm by hitting a hollow wooden block called a moktok that made a tock-tock-tock sound like a woodpecker on a hollow tree. A huge pileated woodpecker swooped in and landed on a dead pine tree just a few feet away looking for the intruder into his territory. Later, moving slowly and quietly, trying to keep the verbal thinking mind as quiet as possible, I sat, walked, sat, and walked inside the black gum swamp as the sun rose. A flock of vultures was eating something but as I approached, they clambered into trees with a great flapping of wings and croaking. It was a young coyote and the birds had already picked the bones nearly clean. The dirty hide was a limp blanket over them. Wild animals rarely live long enough to experience aging and degenerative diseases like cancer but when they die, it's usually quick. Predators are fast, life is short and death comes soon. Humans don't have to fend off so many attacks from predators so we often end up old and feeble for years. Who has the better deal, I wondered.

A slender little black snake with two sky-blue racing stripes darted past my knee. It was a blue-striped ribbon snake, a subspecies that occurs only in wet coastal areas between Florida's Withlacoochee and Ochlockonee Rivers. Not only was it beautiful, it was an endemic, one whose only home on Earth was right here in this swampy coastal forest. Science is a powerful method for understanding the reality in which we live. Its strength comes from the ability to join the observations of many different individuals into a coherent view. The fruits of many lifetimes of work are stored in back issues of technical journals. At my fingertips was all the work, all the insights of thousands of other scientists I'd never met. The brief description of the blue-striped ribbon snake (it eats small fish and amphibians) represented years of prowling the same woods and collecting by some herpetologist I'd never meet. He probably loved the beauty of the palm forest as much as I did.

Traditional practice emphasizes reducing sensory input by staring at the floor in a silent space and remaining motionless. Instead I filled the senses with nature, filling eyes with sun glitter on water, filling the ears with wind in trees and birdsong. Nature doesn't engage human ego. It also creates the necessary state of humility and unknowing until there is no separation and you are part of it. Words are labels for the human ideas we make, but Reality is wordless in the forest or the sea. Dropping words allows us to directly experience that wordlessness beneath the surface of labeled name and form. The mind is like a mirror that engages with what appears before it. A mirror, however, is not encrusted with a thick coating of old habitual reflections. Our minds usually are coated with old thoughts and emotions. Not thinking can eventually lead to a clear mind that isn't coated with old thoughts. Then what we experience is a gateway to something different from everyday reality. When we continue to experience normal sensory input but without the usual running commentary and labeling of everything, a new perception of reality may arise. On rare occasions, sensory input may also disappear, revealing further mental states.

After a week, however, the honeymoon was over. Big biting yellow flies had hatched out by the millions and my blood was the key to hatching their next generation. The flimsy screen tent didn't begin to keep them out. An entomologist later explained that they go to a contrasting visual pattern and strongly prefer blue or green colors. Once they hit a vertical surface, they crawl down. My tent had a green stripe around it and sure enough, the flying killerbots hit the side and then moved down to the bottom where the loose flaps directed them into the tent and then to the meat – me. My carefully prepared screen pavilion was a sieve, a yellow fly trap and I was the bait. Their bites caused red allergenic welts. And I was eaten alive by chiggers, filthy, sweaty, stinky and sleeping naked because it made the chigger bites less miserable. An unstoppable assault by ticks required constant mindfulness to feel and remove them before they could dig in. The only way to survive outside the tent was to wear a veiled broad-brim hat and clothes over all bare skin. Being under constant itchy assault produced a lot of mental restlessness. A forest may be beautiful but insects are completely ruthless in meeting their needs. What did the Buddha do about bugs? Did biting flies live in those Himalayan foothills where he practiced? If Buddha had lived in swampy hot buggy Florida, Buddhism would probably never have appeared, I thought sourly.

As I became more and more restless, indoors looked better and better. I started to fantasize about bathtubs and air conditioning. I felt guilty about all the things I was leaving undone at work and at home. And I missed seeing my family and friends. I liked the idea of a solo retreat in a forest, but how did I like the reality of it? Why on earth was I doing this? Perhaps the lesson of so much time in the forest was only that a fulfilling life for a human is to be found with other humans??? The Buddha spent a long time alone in forest, got something, and then came back into human society.

Life is for doing, for taking action and needs the correct balance of action and stillness. Sitting in woods was beginning to seem like too much stillness. Or maybe it was unfolding just fine and there was no need to be frustrated about it not happening some other way. Zen practice, according to one teacher I had sat a retreat with, meant having confidence in a mind that is free of knowing, but we are uncomfortable with that so we try to organize the world of our experience into labeled categories, seeking a sense of control. Do not do this, he advised, but stay in the openness of not understanding. Each short retreat was one step on a long path. It was important work but did it really require living in a swamp with no plumbing?

When a swarm of huge horse flies, between one and two inches long, landed on the screen, I bailed out and went home to get more bricks to weight down the tent flaps. There was no defense except to smack them, but killing the flies was not only the taking of life, which broke a basic Buddhist precept, it also kept the mind locked into ego-based problem-solving mode trying to preserve its hide, trying to fix the tent so the flies couldn't get inside, evaluating the fixes which mostly didn't work. The extra bricks took care of 80% of the problem but one single fly was all it took to destroy meditation. It was impossible for the mind to settle and I couldn't clear the flies out anyway. Problem solving about flies and brush, roaming about in the car to implement solutions, evaluating the results which failed, all the control issues of the ego were the opposite of a meditative state. When the misery seemed intolerable, a little toad somehow got inside the tent and sat with me. Utterly motionless, it breathed calmly in and out. Its bright calm eyes and fluttering throat seemed to be teaching me how to live in this insect-swarming world. It was better at sitting than a cat. A human wasn't even close.

The next evening two wood ducks were foraging in the cypress pond in front of the tent. I moved around as little as possible and they stayed. After sunset, several more swooped in, passing only a few feet overhead. Walking around the backside of the pond in the last light before full darkness, after the flies had quit patrolling, I startled a big flock of robins. Their flight flushed the wood ducks out of the pond, and where I had thought there were ten, at least twenty-five or thirty thundered overhead from the pond to the main lake. Swarms of lightning bugs flashed incessantly, as intense as a strobe show, so bright they lit up the ground with each flash. The show lasted for about an hour and when it ended there was only the star-spangled tree canopy and one bullfrog way off in the distance. As it got darker, the big oaks took on a sharp glittering beauty, with stars on every branch like Christmas trees.

Later on the night turned foggy and rainy. The bedding got wet and I was too cold to focus on anything except being cold and very dirty. The tent was full of sand and leaves and I couldn't sweep it out. After a night on a half-inflated air mattress, I was aching all over by morning. With almost no sleep plus a severe diet, I could hardly move the next morning. My nose ran incessantly and I was so weak from inadequate food that it was nearly impossible to do work practice which consisted that day of picking up acorns and throwing them in the cypress pond for the wood ducks. That afternoon, a heavy rain fell and the normally black surface of the cypress pond was white and silvery from the impact of the raindrops. The whole area seemed much more open and bright than in sunlight. A squirrel jumped off a limb of a wet bush in the cypress pond, and a sudden silver circle sparkled in weak sunlight on the water below. Every wind gust sent a shower of black gum and red maple leaves and acorns from the tall water oaks around the pond to the ground. Still straight reflections of cypress in the pond danced when a water strider skated by. Throwing acorns into water for ducks to harvest more easily would seem crazy anywhere else but here it made sense. The rules were different in this realm.

As the nights passed, I felt more and more uneasy sitting alone on the ground in the dark. No primate had willingly done this in millions of years, ever since humans mastered fire. Before that, our ancestors doubtless slept in trees after dark. Sitting there was maybe more than a little dumb given that I had seen panthers near here and panthers would easily attack something no bigger than a seated human. I retreated to the tent. It might be flimsy but it looked big. That was better until ungodly howls came from the lake. Barred owls screech, cackle and howl. Maybe it was an exceptionally maniacal barred owl but it didn't quite sound like that. A thunderhead full of brilliant white-and-blue heat lightning slowly approached from the south off the Gulf. A single crash of lightning suddenly struck and rain poured for about thirty minutes.

Sleep and wakefulness alternated on most nights but there was not much sleep. Lying alone in a dark forest, like any serious spiritual practice, meant facing the personal demons of loss, anger and fear that all of us carry in some form, either consciously or subconsciously. They always came most strongly at night when other issues and distractions were minimal. Such fear arises regardless of any intellectual ideas, opinions or religious beliefs about the situation. Unlike the imaginary woods monsters, those fears would not go away just because I acknowledged them or wished that they would. They came from attachment to Anne, her survival and her quality of life.

At a recent weekend Zen retreat, the teacher had said "If we experience loss 100%, it is the loss and grief of all beings and we move from reactive bitterness to great compassion, to intense aliveness and to great love/great sorrow. That place of brightness, aliveness, clarity and goodness is one's own True Nature. We can only experience it in the present tense. When doing what you love, in that moment you are resourceful, creative and alive and the doing of it is the meaning of life. We will take risks in service of it – it is not duty or obligation. So Zen practice means to slow down, rest the mind, remove the gap between the self and what is happening and experience the aliveness of the moment. You have to clarify and solve your situation before you can let it go and get beyond it - try to skip that step and it'll just keep tripping you up."

Who is afraid? I asked myself lying there in the dark. I am! What am I? What exactly am I afraid of? Anger about an old sense of betrayal suddenly appeared as it had done a thousand times before. I knew that situation was a place to practice the Biblical teaching of turning the other cheek but had never been able to attain it. Suddenly I knew that the point of practicing turn the other check is that the only alternative is to drag around the burden of anger, grief, bitterness and hostility that arises after such an attack. That is the most self-destructive thing we can do because it ruins our own chance of experiencing peace of mind and the wellbeing and happiness that can only arise out of a peaceful mind. Turning the other cheek means to live a life of mental as well as physical nonviolence, a practice that is essential to experience the peaceful mind that is the foundation for a life of wellbeing. There is no personal mental peace without forgiveness and there is no joy or happiness without a peaceful mind.

The Korean Zen master Kyong Ho once said that great trees have great uses and small trees have small uses. Find the proper use of a good situation, find the proper use of a bad situation, he said, don't attach to the good or push away the bad but make the situation correct. As a child, I had tried over and over to float in the shallow water at the beach, but every time I tried to relax, I would sink until my face was covered and then leap in a panic back onto my feet. One day I finally realized that the water was only 4 feet deep and even if I sank to the bottom, I only had to stand up again so there was no way to drown if I would just relax and trust the situation. As soon as I did that I began to float.

Having learned how to float, it becomes possible to live in a place of open-ended discovery of what is regardless of whether "what is" was what I wanted it to be. The only answer was to really know that there is a larger-scale pattern to life, that it's not all about being an isolated individual alone in the universe.

An invisible deer went crashing through the palmetto and waded across the cypress pond. Then a snarl in the dark sounded like a big cat near the camp. Was that a panther? It came again and it was clearly a cat type snarl and too loud to be a bobcat. A rumble of distant thunder from the departing storm rolled overhead. Could the snarl have just been thunder? The thunder came from the west and the snarl was off to the east. If there was a panther nearby, this solo camping in the forest might not be safe but if it was thunder and an overactive imagination, then the situation was just silly.

I thought about those monks who had wandered alone in virgin tropical forests that had tigers, wild elephants and huge pythons. The key to surviving an encounter with a large dangerous animal was to stay calm which required mental focus. Facing a tiger alone led to intense fear and sometimes that fear opened the door to a radically different understanding of Reality that suddenly produced a clear and bright mind of inner peace and unshakable courage.

"If you are terrified of tigers, be where tigers are and make friends with them" said one master in this tradition. "Let go of attachment to life itself then there is no fear of death."

Those monks believed that it was possible to establish a mind to mind connection to request the animal to be calm.

"From such a mind…the tiger, snake or elephant will draw back – one may be able to walk up to it based on metta (loving kindness or benevolence) which has a real and profound influence - the animals feel and sense it – the mysterious power of mind…is self-evident but difficult for others to realize who have not yet developed it."

"The damma (Truth) is on the other side of death – without crossing that threshold (fear of death) there is no hope of realizing the damma. If you don't practice, you won't know," he continued.

Without denying or minimizing the fear, I tried to balance it with conscious gratitude for the many positive aspects of life that more than equaled life's physical and mental tigers. No matter how difficult life may be in any given moment, it is always possible to look more closely at the tiniest details of life and find something to be grateful for. That in turn creates the possibility of being able to act with poise, dignity and total attention, of engaging others with loving kindness. Eventually the night racket in the forest settled into stillness. With gratitude for that, I fell into a restless troubled sleep full of bad dreams.

Suddenly I awoke and sat up. Outside the tent window, the first red light was a narrow band on the eastern horizon. Turning my head, I was suddenly nose to nose with a black bear standing quietly a few inches away on the other side of another window. Only a flimsy nylon window screen was between us. The bear's ears were amazingly huge. I never realized bears have such big ears, I thought to myself slowly.

"Hello bear, I hope you don't eat people," I said as politely as I could manage. We continued to stare at each other in silence for another minute and then the bear jumped backwards. He (she?) turned and gazed at me again and we resumed the silent staring contest. Then the bear swung around and slowly ran off. About 20 feet away, he or she stopped for a last long look and then disappeared into the forest. Many Native Americans believe that bears are bearers of great power and are associated with dreams and healing. I knew I would be talking to a native teacher about this as soon as I got home.

Sitting still wasn't an option after that so I took a long walk on a dirt road that went past a house a mile away from the camp. The sound of a TV blew away the last remnants of my composure. To be deep in the woods is hugely different than to be on even the smallest dirt road. The human order imposed by the road, its edges and apartness from what is on either side creates a sense of separation from the functioning landscape, destroys a sense of connectedness that could otherwise flow. Its linearity destroys the integrity of the biological fabric. Nature avoids straight lines. I stomped back to camp and fixed breakfast.

On the last evening of the retreat I built a campfire. By dark it was down to red glowing pockets in wet peat. The peat kept smoldering and there was no water to douse the fire. Hot spots flared up, grew larger, faded out then reappeared. Any one of them had the potential to burn the forest down if conditions were right for that to happen. I didn't want to leave the fire unattended so I tried to sleep on the ground, sharing a sleeping bag with the dog from down the road that occasionally came to visit. Between the two of us, we could stay warm. It was a good place to be. There was no mental noise from other human minds here. The trees were sentient in a way that floor boards and electric lights in a house are not sentient. Finally the air turned cold, dew appeared and the fire died.

AT SEA

Solo meditation at sea, even close to
shore, has an edge to it that is not part of
sitting in a temple. There is no room for
the mental cobwebs of restlessness and
dissatisfaction.

The little boat pitched and tossed on its anchor line like a wild horse under a purple and black sky in front of a remote marshy island in the northern Gulf of Mexico. The idea had been to spend some time meditating alone on the island, but the sea was too rough to even think about wading ashore.

The last time I'd been there, fifteen ospreys were hunting in the blue and yellow and silver morning, little spider crabs were busy on a sand flat doing who knows what, and a hidden fairy grove of green trees and blue flowers paved the ground on the island with the sunlit blue sea glittering through the leaves. This time, my analytical thinking mind urgently pointed out that I was there with a broken rusty anchor, no bail cup, and no fresh water. I hadn't checked the tide or weather radar before leaving. I hadn't even told anybody that I was going. I broke every safety rule in the book.

Solo meditation at sea, even close to shore, has an edge to it that is not part of sitting in a temple. It means being totally in this moment and alert to what is needed. There is no room for the mental cobwebs of restlessness and dissatisfaction. Although the Zen tradition emphasizes the impermanent transient nature of a human life and challenges us to perceive the reality that is beyond birth and death, I quickly realized that I didn't really want to drown on this particular afternoon. The weather worsened until I barely had the strength and energy to pull the anchor against a stiff wind and chop, but as I got underway and was running back to port, I felt alive and strong. Time and space both flowed freely.

The next day I went back to sea with a much better prepared collecting crew from our aquarium to dive for sponges and sea whips further offshore. The storm had passed and the sea was silken flat and pastel baby blue. There was no horizon as the sea blended with the sky in the far distance. Ducks, gulls and pelicans were everywhere and a sponge forest had grown up on what had been bare rock a year before.

A limestone outcrop on the sea floor was covered with yellow soft corals and bright orange sponges. Silversides, spots, grunts, hogfish, parrotfish, and a school of 5 huge tarpon kept a discrete distance while a 5 foot spotted eagle ray swam over the rocks, its tubular mouth vacuuming the rock and its two wing tips pointed straight up. Red and green parrotfish, big filefish and mangrove snappers picked among the rocks. A school of silvery look downs passed by, undulating back and forth in sinuous movements. Lying quietly amidst the rubble two brown nurse sharks tried to hide.

Amidst them a young green turtle cruised along. Maybe fourteen inches long, the sunrise pattern of yellow and brown streaks on the shell was perfect camouflage against the bottom of rock, sponge, coral and sand patches. It half swam, half crawled over the rocks, head down, tearing algae off the bottom. Every move was perfection, a blending into the water. That effortless soaring flight, banking and tilting with slow relaxed strokes was a total contrast to the heavy crawl of nesting females on the beach. Who would have thought they were such free and graceful creatures, flying underwater, rising vertically to the surface to breathe?

I followed it for a while, my awkward flippers thrusting, pounding, swimming as best I could, while it moved effortlessly away, headed for deeper water. The turtle steadily winged its way off the reef, out over the white sand bottom, until it put on a burst of speed and left me behind.

Some rocks were covered with a bushy brown clump about 3- to 4 inches high. Although it looked like some kind of drab seaweed, it wasn't a plant at all. Each clump was an obscure invertebrate animal called *Bugula neritina*. A member of a group of animals called bryozoans that filter microscopic food out of seawater, it grows as a colony of individuals that lack head, legs, eyes, etc. With neither the ability to move nor claws to defend itself, a colony ought to be a tasty snack for browsing fish but it's not. It protects itself chemically, synthesizing potent biochemical compounds toxic to would-predators.

Even though I had known of the bryozoan species for years, I had never looked at it under a dissecting microscope until recently. When I did, it had been a dazzling trip into a world of life forms I'd never seen before. Each microscopic individual in the colony repeatedly expanded an elegant bell-shaped set of feeding tentacles. Each tentacle had even smaller beating cilia that pulled a water current through the crown. They would occasionally twitch and withdraw as the tiny currents pulled in a algal cell. On some colonies — which looked the same superficially but turned out to be members of another, closely related, species — little cleaning structures that looked like a bird's beak flicked up and down like a precision clockwork mechanism.

Microscopic one-eyed crustaceans, now invisible to my diver's eye, carried their eggs on their tails as they had sailed around the colony's branches like darting swallows. Whizzing protozoans, tiny worms browsing over green and red algae sprouts, created an incredibly busy universe. A relatively huge spinning oval- shaped creature hovered like a mysterious alien spaceship, surrounded by an electric-blue halo created by light refracting off of its beating cilia. Released from the parent colony in the ocean, the embryonic bryozoan would drift until it found just the right type of surface and then settle down to grow into a Y-shaped baby colony with just a few feeding individuals. The colony would then grow and fork and branch, producing more genetically identical individuals until it resembled its parent.

I had sat there and stared at it all asking

"What is this? Don't know! WHAT ON EARTH IS THIS!?"

For years I had lectured to university marine biology students, drawn diagrams on blackboards, in general taking bryozoans for granted and acted like I understood them. But I'd never really looked, never really paid attention and so I'd never truly seen them. The marvelousness of life on Earth, the absolute mystery of what it ultimately is, how it comes to be, was all there. All I had to do is look.

Zen starts with questions: "What on earth is this?" is as good as any. What is reality? What am I? And it emphasizes personal exploration and discovery to resolve these questions. The answers to such questions are found not in any particular founding myth or revealed truth, but in what we can observe and experience directly when the mind shifts into a non-verbal state of awareness.

To reach that point one holds the question "what is this?" in mind in an open ended way, not settling for a quick superficial analytical answer but always looking deeper and deeper into the question. Lying on the sea floor, staring at the bryozoan colonies, the only answer that arose was "I don't know" but that don't know is an invitation to further exploration and discovery.

After working offshore for a few hours, we moved to an inshore sea grass meadow and dove there. The underwater turtle grass beds of the Florida Gulf Coast are a separate universe, only a few feet from the more familiar terrestrial landscape of beaches. It was a world of white sand shining between bright green blades of grass, of lacy piles of golden- and rose-colored algae floating past. Four species of flowering marine grasses grew together, creating food and shelter for hundreds of species of fish and invertebrates. Red sponges, red starfish and red sea anemones accentuated the green and white seascape.

Here, a lot of the animals remained motionless while the world in which they lived was in constant movement. All of these other species had been totally hidden and invisible to a human diver's eye. Darting hordes of pinfish and pigfish flashed gold and azure blue pinstripes on silver bodies as they darted about. Their bottomless black eyes were ringed with solid gold. The fish swam just above the grass tops, occasionally dropping below to nose in the sand. Why didn't they eat the swarming shrimp? Efficient visual hunters, they routinely picked even smaller amphipod crustaceans off the grass blades, so surely they could see the shrimp.

The meadow was full of tiny emerald green snails that none of us had ever seen before. Comb jellyfish flashed red, yellow and green in the afternoon sun on a falling tide. A round black-and-yellow spiny boxfish came swimming slowly through the darting hordes of pinfish like a blimp. It inspected me almost thoughtfully and then wandered on. Why so few of them, so incredibly many pinfish? While I puzzled over that one, a school of menhaden swept past in perfect symmetry and order.

Toadfish mating whistles beeped like sea buoys all around. Spiny red sea urchins were everywhere, the little ones up and entwined in the grass, the big ones sitting on the sand under umbrellas of shells they held over themselves for shade. The urchins were the round red spiny cows of this pasture. They grazed microscopic algae off the grass blades. One small urchin nestled into the broken shell of its great great grandparent ancestor of the year before. Another moved slowly past, its spines madly whirling in all directions. It carried white shells perched above its spines like a lady in a big hat and seemed almost a being from another world.

Patches of scarlet red beard sponge grew everywhere on mussel shells and baby octopus hid in the empty mussel shells. Brown spider crabs, blue-eyed scallops, and orange pen shell clams were everywhere. One spider crab sat motionless with her eyestalks rotated back in her head. Was she asleep? Do crabs sleep? I touched her, she swiveled her eyes up to have a look and scrambled away.

It was awesomely beautiful and the joy of simply being alive and present grew and grew to a thunderous level. Suddenly my consciousness shifted into a physical experience of no separation, no independent self apart from the ocean. Human bones and muscles moving through the water were as much a part of that ecosystem and that place and moment as were the fish and the sea grass. Any sense of human or personal distinctiveness disappeared. The human was just part of the fauna in that moment, and "I" didn't exist. It wasn't an idea, it was physical reality and the entire universe was there, totally complete and whole and alive. That awareness unfolded like a budding flower, beginning to open into something even bigger, something transcendent. It absolutely needed silence and solitude to continue to unfold but the other divers were waving me back to the boat. As soon as there was the sound of words and voices, the unfolding stopped and I was again a separate human being swimming in the ocean. A strong wordless sense of the underlying perfection of everything persisted for hours afterwards. It had arisen out of joy and gratitude.

A few weeks later, I was at sea again with the students in a marine biology class that was part of a university continuing education program for adults. On deck 20 people, a mixture of school teachers, state agency staffers and business people relaxed and enjoyed the view as we headed about 10 miles offshore in the 45-foot R/V Seminole, a slow but powerful and seaworthy vessel that could carry an entire class. Many of them had never been offshore before and it was an adventure that they would remember for years to come. What they would learn about marine life would be vivid and alive instead of tedious text book illustrations. I hoped that the firsthand experience would spark a commitment to pre-serving nature. It's hard to care about something that you have never experienced first-hand.

We planned to pull bottom fishing nets on the sea floor of the continental shelf. Standing on a beach looking out to sea seems like standing at the edge of the world, peering into nothingness but that is an illusion. The beach is not the edge of the continent. That lies miles offshore in about 600 feet of water where the continent plunges down into the abyssal depths of the ocean basins. The outer edge of the continent is alternately exposed as dry land and covered over as sea floor as sea level rises and falls over geologic time. The part that's dry at a given time is called the coastal plain and the submerged area from the low tide explored by beachcombers to the deep edge explored by research submersibles is the continental shelf.

The sky was overcast but the weather forecast was fine —light wind. It was good news. This trip had been canceled twice already because of small craft warnings that had then dissolved into sunny calm weather that wouldn't faze a canoe. An hour later, the Seminole slid easily over the swells, its net dragging the bottom 40 feet below. Continental shelf bottoms are huge expanses of sand or mud bottom with scattered rock ledges breaking the surface of the sand. These rock bottoms are the equivalent of rich oases in the relatively more sparsely populated sand or mud plains. Sponges and soft corals, bryozoans and algae wave in the currents. Sponges dominate, sometimes contributing three-fourths of the total community by weight. Fishes swarm around the outcrops, feeding on the myriads of tiny crustaceans, worms and other species that hide in the large colonies of filter feeders.

Above the bottom, the three dimensional world of the water column supports another community of life. Schools of predatory mackerel and jacks, plankton-filtering menhaden and other fishes, rainbow-colored darting squid, marine mammals and sea turtles soar through the space between the bottom and the surface. Jellyfish pulse like flashing zeppelins, engulfing and devouring tiny crustaceans and fish that are touched by their stinging tentacles. Directly or indirectly, all of these species depend on the microscopic floating world of the plankton for food. The species that swim above the bottom either filter plankton out of the water or prey on those that do.

The sediments are also alive with their own community of plants and animals. Burrowing species of sea cucumbers, clams, snails, polychaete worms, and crustaceans build burrows and pump food and oxygen-rich surface water through them, remaining safe from most of their potential predators. Near the surface of the sediment, microscopic crustaceans and worms, shelled amoebas and single- celled plants live between the sand grains, moving around between transparent quartz boulders. The concentration of these tiny creatures can range from 50,000 to 1 million individuals per square meter in coastal areas. And, best of all, aside from fisheries and coral reefs, and despite all the above facts and figures, we really know almost nothing about most of the species that live out there. There's a lot of discovering still waiting to be done.

When the net emerged from the sea, showering water on the deck, we had basket stars and crabs, sponges and shrimp and scallops. Eels snaked through the pile and croakers croaked. We quickly sorted them in buckets of sea water to keep them alive while we looked at them.

Mixed in with the crabs, starfish and small fishes were a dozen pancake shaped tan electric rays with big brown spots. While all sharks, rays and catfish species can detect electric fields produced by the muscles and nerves of other organisms, only a few species can generate and control larger electric fields. In the ocean, electric rays use electricity to zap their predators and stun their prey.

A medical researcher at the Howard Hughes Medical Institute was using electric rays to study the biochemistry of acetylcholine, one of many neurotransmitters in mammalian nervous systems. In humans, problems with acetylcholine are involved in serious diseases such as myasthenia gravis. In order to have any hope of treating such conditions, a better understanding of the biochemistry involved was essential. The rays' electric organs are powered solely by acetylcholine so they are a good model to explore the biochemical pathways whereby that neurotransmitter is created, used and eliminated at nerve synapses.

We gently placed the ones we needed for the researcher into bags with water and oxygen. We then tagged and released the rest to learn more about their distribution and migrations. Unlike almost all other fish that depend on speed to survive, the tagged rays swam slowly down into the depths. Suddenly a six foot shark materialized beside a ray like a menacing gray apparition, scrutinized it with the rapt attention of the hungry, but then faded back into the shadowy murk without attacking. Two porpoises came rocketing up from beneath the boat, their mouths wide open, ready to swallow it. They got within two feet of the ray, then broke off the attack in unison, veered sharply and fled. The ray seemed to discharge its electric organs when it perceived a big predator closing in. If it waited until it was bitten before discharging, it would be too late, we had always assumed, until we found a live healthy ray with a semicircular set of dents on its body from a shark bite that had been stopped in the midst of slamming the jaws together.

In the ocean life and death encounters are non-stop – it's simply how the system works. Humans, on the other hand, tend to be afraid of death and cling to this lifetime. A major goal of Zen meditation is to transcend that fear and at the same time learn to experience each moment of life richly and intensely. Japanese Zen trained samurai used their training to cultivate fearlessness in battle. Today, many Zen teachers still test their students' attainment and insight with a challenging debate form called dharma combat, a verbal form of the old swordsmen's thrust and parry.

The seas were beginning to pick up a bit — an occasional whitecap flashed by — so we decided to make only one more short drag and then run back inshore to work off the beach. Behind the big submerged sand bar that stretched out from the beach, it would be calm enough to resume collecting. By the time the net hit the deck again, the sea was distinctly rough and we quickly turned toward shore. Students just don't get excited about the biology of starfish when their stomachs start swilling toward their ears and mouths.

Then the captain picked up a faint, broken, almost-inaudible radio distress call. It was a 23-foot speedboat with a broken motor. The name didn't come through but after several tries, we got the boat's position — it was miles further offshore. At our slow pace we were several hours away, but nobody else on the radio was closer and it was now so rough that no smaller boat was willing to try it — this one was ours.

With a crew of increasingly seasick marine biology students, we turned the bow back out to sea. After forever, a tiny white speck showed up on radar and then became visible. The little boat was pitching violently on its anchor line, not far from sinking with three men aboard. After several passes we got close enough to catch their tow line. I grabbed it, ran it back to the stern and hastily fastened it to the cleat. It was too rough to attempt to transfer the men so they hunkered down for their Nantucket sleigh ride and we started the long beating trip back to shore. By now the seas were 6-to-8 feet and the students were comatose, draped over bunks and collecting buckets, marine biology a bad dream. The heavy, water-filled buckets with our animals started to slide back and forth across the heaving deck so I grabbed a rope and staggered and lurched over to try and lash them against the rail. As I bent over, the too thin tow line to the other boat snapped and lashed around my back twice with the force of a 2 by 4.

"Are you all right?" somebody shouted.

"No!" I gasped and staggered out of the way as the captain circled back to try and pick them up again. Nobody else could move safely on the rolling deck so after catching my breath, I got back to the rail, caught the line and secured it again. When the fishermen radioed our captain asking if we could slow down so they could fish, we exchanged speechless expressions of disbelief. They seemed to have no idea of how much danger they were in or maybe they were in some state of bravado based denial. When we offered to cast off the tow and leave them to fish, they quickly sobered up.

Unlike shallow coastal marshes and sea grass meadows, the continental shelf is open ocean, a place where those without sufficient skills, experience and equipment can and do die from time to time. Yet both biologists and fishermen head out there daily because that's where the action is. Continental shelves have only 10 percent of the ocean's surface, but these productive edges yield 30 percent of the ocean's life. If you want to really understand what life on this planet is, how many ways there really are to build an animal or a plant, you have to go to the continental shelf because that is where most life is. Life first appeared and diversified in the ocean, and most of it never left.

Land was on the horizon when the line snapped again. One more time we circled back and got the fishermen. A small boat from the marina finally met us at the outer channel marker and picked up the tow. The fishermen didn't even thank us for the rescue.

After handing off the fishermen to the marina's boat, we were back in more sheltered waters. A few of the students began to feel better and came out on deck to look at the catch during the ride back to the university marine station dock. Nearly all the plants and animals that inhabit land are members of only three lineages that successfully made the transition from sea to land — the vascular plants, the insects and the vertebrates. Yet there are altogether approximately 35 major groups called phyla of animals and 14 of plants. Most of them occur predominantly or even exclusively in the ocean. Lots of things that appear to be alive somehow aren't recognizable as any familiar animals - bushy masses that look like plants but aren't green; orange or yellow lumps that resemble rubber with little pink spots. At night the water may glow with an eerie blue light. What is all this stuff? A closer look at the eminently successful alternate life styles that these animals represent provides a more accurate view of what life on earth really is.

A 2 foot long horse conch, a snail with a bright orange foot, had come part way out of its massive shell and was slowly climbing up the inside of one of the larger buckets. It was a mollusk, one of the group that also includes clams, octopus, squid and thousands of other tiny species that only biologists even know exist. When we think of mollusks (if we think of them at all), we might think of a clam or an oyster, a few primitive creatures crawling low upon the earth. In fact mollusks are the second largest, second most successful group of large animals on earth with about 110,000 species. It's just that almost half of their 90,000 species of snails, 90 percent of their 15,000 species of clams and all of their other species are in the ocean where most of us never see them. Aquatic arthropods – crabs, shrimp, barnacles, microscopic copepods and so on - have more than twice as many species as do mollusks.

To put these numbers in perspective, the group that includes the vertebrates — the fishes, frogs, lizards and turtles, the birds and furry mammals - all of the forms that are displayed in our zoos and we humans as well — are only about 50,000 species strong. There are about as many sponge species as there are mammals. And yet we arrogantly classify animals into vertebrates and invertebrates — 50,000 species versus millions of species that are lumped together as "not us vertebrates." And worse, we assume that those millions of diverse and successful forms of life are somehow inferior because their bodies don't happen to have a backbone like ours do. If we measure biological success by the ability to alter the planet to suit ourselves, then humans are unquestionably the most successful species. But if we use species number, which measures the successful evolutionary diversification of a biological lineage into different species living in different habitats, the single species of humans or even the handful of primate species doesn't amount to much.

Wait a minute, you say! How can anyone compare the species that perceives the divine to an insect or a clam? What about the human intellect, our culture? What about Mozart and McDonald's, the computer, art and football? Marine invertebrate creatures that lack complex individual minds are merely a backdrop to our own glory!

If we judge biological success by sheer inventiveness, then the relative numbers don't mean so much. Human intellect and culture are endlessly wonderful. It's just that there are other ways to judge success, like species number. If we use that approach, the picture of life on earth that emerges is vastly different from the human-centered image we take for granted.

Many Korean Zen temples explicitly celebrate nature. The temple grounds are often forests and nature preserves. The exterior walls are covered with images of flowers, birds and tigers. Stone and wood carvings of elephants, tortoises, tigers, fish, cranes and dragons may surround the Buddha statue on the altar. Human mind reaches toward transcendence surrounded and supported by all of the living world rather than being separated from it.

Modern humans have been around for maybe as little as a hundred thousand years. The ancestry of the horseshoe crabs in our collecting buckets went back at least 400 million years. Ancient massive cousins of scorpions and spiders with huge shells and dagger like tails or telsons, horseshoe crabs are living fossils, little changed in those 400 million years. I had done many years of research on the behavioral ecology of the crabs. In one part of the work, teams of volunteers had tagged and released ten thousand crabs. I had then spent month after month on horseshoe crab breeding beaches hiking for miles looking for tagged crabs. Horseshoe crabs nest every spring on Atlantic and Gulf beaches. They come to the beach to nest only on high tides around the full or new moons, when the tides are the highest of the month, protecting the eggs from aquatic predators. Night tides have more crabs than afternoon tides.

A few weeks before this offshore field trip, I had gone to one local horseshoe crab breeding beach on a full moon at 3 AM to see how many crabs were coming ashore locally after a massive oil spill the previous summer. We were east of the main effects but not very far east. Were they ok, or had their populations been decimated?

On the first nesting moon of the season, I had not expected to see more than a few dozen. It was windy and the crabs were having a tough time, flipping over in the surf, but there were hundreds there in a short stretch of beach, digging into the sand to lay and fertilize eggs, insuring the next generation in their ancient lineage.

After so many these years, there wasn't a single crab with a tag. They were as naked as they were before all that tagging work. Ancient creatures that have been around since long before the dinosaurs appeared, their span on earth is incomprehensible to a single finite human mind. The project that had been so important in my life years before was gone without a trace, as ephemeral and impermanent as a single wave breaking on the shore. For that matter, so was I. The tags were all gone and in a few years I would be equally gone and forgotten.

As I had walked the silent beach alone in the moonlight for several miles, time and events broke into smaller and smaller pieces, with the mind focusing on each one of them, experiencing each moment with total focus. Now is the time to step over a log. Stepping over the log. Then is the time to take this step. Moving the leg forward. Then is the time to sit down. Sitting down. Then….. Etc, etc. Mindfulness wasn't an abstract Zen ideal, it was simply how the brain physically shifted into a different way of functioning, measuring the night by time to walk, time to sit, time to rest.

We abstract time by labeling the hours of the day and the days of the week. Dividing our days into hours and minutes, we create an artificial mental scaffolding of schedules to keep and tasks to do. We label the cycle of seasons and number the years, creating a sense of progression and linear time, but each unique named day of the labeled month of the numbered year is only a mental abstraction, a human idea superimposed on the endless cyclic alternation of darkness and light and seasonal weather patterns.

Daylight and darkness have alternated nonstop for billions of years. There is only the still silent passage of the sun and moon overhead over and over again as the earth spins on its axis, only the changing light and colors as sun, moon and stars pass across the sky. There is no new day, only the endless cyclic alternation of light and dark, cold and hot, wet and dry weather, activity and rest. In the morning daylight simply resumes. It is not a new day. This timeless space has existed for billions of years.

All caught up in the world of thinking and personal identity, we mostly don't notice that the nonverbal cyclic time that underlies the calendar even exists. Go back through enough sunrises and sunsets and everybody would be wearing different clothes and using different technology, but there would be no gap between then and this very moment. Horseshoe crabs time their actions to the cyclic waxing and waning of the moon. They've been doing it for hundreds of millions of years as humans count time but to the crab perhaps there is only right now.

"The distinction between past, present and future is only an illusion," said Einstein. This moment, this night was not separate from the moment when the first living thing appeared. Endless time had become timeless.

Back in the here and now of the collecting trip, we released our horseshoe crabs into the sea along with the rest of the catch as the captain turned the bow of the Seminole toward home, back to the more familiar world of dry land, vertebrates, plants, insects and human beings. That night, the wind blew at near gale force. Those fishermen we had towed in were lucky to be alive. If their broken up radio transmission hadn't gotten through, they never would have seen the sun rise again.

CHAPTER 3

SAVING SOME SENTIENT BEINGS

Sentient beings are numberless.
We vow to save them all.

Zen Bodhisattva Vow

I hadn't gotten to the swamp camp site in over a year due to endless other work obligations and family issues. Finally some clear space appeared when the kids went to camp and Jack was out of town. The wind dancing and gusting through the trees was the forest breathing as I headed out to the forest camp. Big clouds floated in a pink evening sky on a hot evening.

Next to the lake at my retreat site, the five acre front field of tall sparse planted pine and grass was far from a virgin wilderness. An old farm field 100 years before, it had been planted in pines 50 years later. With no controlled burning for the last fifty years, the scrub oak and vines had then become an impenetrable thicket above barren ground by the time I got it. It was a green desert and I wanted to restore it to something like a native forest.

At formal meditation retreats, we vowed every day to save all sentient beings in one of the many paradoxes of the Zen tradition. Taken literally, it seems like an impossible absurdity but even as we destroy wild lands and gopher tortoises, a tiny handful of biologists are trying to heal some of the damage. On public lands, on Nature Conservancy and academic preserves, restoration ecologists are learning how to germinate key species to do something about the abuse we've heaped on our planet. They're studying the critical role of soil fungi in maintaining other plant species as they attempt to learn how to rebuild wetlands, forests and prairies. The goal is to save at least some sentient beings, those that hover close to extinction.

It's mostly being done by trial and error. You have to know what a site was like centuries ago to know what species should be there now and even that is an arbitrary decision. Humans have always altered their environments. Do we want to approximate the pre-European invasion landscape of a few hundred years ago or the pre human presence landscape of 20,000 years ago. The latter is impossible anyway because the climate is vastly different from what it was then. Life is a moving target, and the face of the earth has changed thousands of times. After defining the target landscape somehow, you have to get the reintroduced species to grow, correct the mistakes, monitor the results, provide for long-term management and fend off developers who would use restoration as an excuse to keep shredding what intact ecosystems are left.

Reintroducing fire for the first time in decades was the initial step in restoring a healthy forest to that field. In the original forest, frequent lightning-set ground fires controlled the oaks and other hardwoods, favoring pines and grasses. Fire is critical to the survival of the ecosystem and all the species that occur in no other environment. There is a Buddhist precept about not setting fires but in my Zen school there was also a rule that said "Know when to keep the precepts and know when to break them," so I felt good to go on that point.

I started burning every few years to eliminate the dense oak scrub and let some sunlight hit the ground. Get the 20-foot-high oak scrub under control, I thought, and then restoring the diverse community of grasses and wild flowers that had once lived there would be easy. Do that, plant native grasses and wildflowers and pretty soon the place would recover, I thought. I'd have hawks and butterflies and — who knows — maybe even a bear down in the swamp.

A natural ecosystem usually has a high degree of organization. The animals and plants have spent millions of years fine-tuning their connection to the physical environment, diversifying into species after species, as they divide up the living space in an efficient way. Plants grow in well-defined zones regulated by gradients of soil type or moisture and species interact in endless ways we don't always understand. Natural ecosystems generally give a sense of harmony and beauty, but the energy flows through a diversity of pathways that are mostly of no immediate benefit to humans. So humans generally create massive alterations in this finely woven fabric, converting them to systems where the energy is diverted into human uses. Pine forests become planted pines, prairies become wheat fields.

Logging, plowing, paving, changing the natural cycles of fire and flood, we disrupt, simplify and bend the world to our own immediate needs. A large percentage of all the sun's energy now flows through such systems. The problem is that most of the time we don't understand the full effects of our changes. There are usually a lot of unintended consequences. The damage is easy to see once you learn how to look. A forest is reduced to brushy thickets that a rabbit can hardly get through; open grassland becomes a semi-desert. As the years pass, the memory of how an environment once looked fades. A new generation doesn't realize what has been lost.

But when I got the burning done and replanted native species, all of the seedlings, some 20 different species, died. Was it my handling or was the soil lacking in some critical nutrient after years of farming followed by more years of neglect? Friends who did this for a living told me that vines always take over after the first fire and they have to be controlled. Burn more frequently at first, they said. But without grass, the pine needles were the only fuel and they took a long time to pile up. Could the vines in their abnormally high densities be releasing some root toxin that kept other species off the site? Nobody knew. The site was a wonderful teacher, but the lessons were about humility.

After five years, I had to admit defeat. After each fire the oaks and vines resprouted from the roots but nothing else seeded in. It was still too shady. The planted pines needed thinning but I'd have to get a logging crew — the trees were too big for me to cut safely. With the help of a forester I had marked about 25 percent of them, but the loggers I called wouldn't touch it — not enough money and too much trouble to bother with. There it sat for almost a year until another forester looked at it. He understood what I was trying to do, but what I had marked for sale wouldn't leave enough room for the feller bunchers and loaders and trucks to work. I needed somebody with a mule, a chainsaw and months to spend on it, but they disappeared a generation ago.

"If we could remark it and take enough little trees to handle the heavy equipment and leave the bigger ones," the forester had said, "you'd have a stand that would look pretty close to what you want but we could afford to do the job."

He had marked a small section, flagging the trees he'd leave so we could see how that might look. A lot would stay but a lot more than I had wanted cut would go.

"Well, I dunno…." I hesitated. It was obvious that nobody was going to do it the way I'd wanted. If I did it and it was too scraggly, I'd have to live with it, but just burning was going nowhere.

"OK," I said, "do it."

A few weeks later the crew moved in, diesels roaring in the unmistakable sound I'd learned to dread over the years, the sound of a forest dying. And this time I did it. But this wasn't a forest, it was a sterile plantation, I reminded myself. And it wasn't a clear-cut.

Nature lovers are called tree huggers but the real tree huggers are loggers using feller bunchers, big yellow machines with giant tires and three claws up front. Looking like giant beetles from hell, they roar up to a tree, hug it in a steel-jawed embrace, cut it at the base and drive it away still upright. They roar and snort like mechanical dinosaurs and down trees faster than I can cut carrots. I could almost feel the trees' terror as the steel-jawed beast hugged them, one after the other. But day by day as the stunted trees had disappeared, leaving spaced- out larger ones, the site looked more and more like a native stand of pine forest. Now, years later, only an expert botanist would know that the site wasn't a native forest. And there were most assuredly bears around.

For this retreat, the plan was to sit as long as I wanted and then to leave. It would be freedom practice – no rigid schedule, no physical struggle to remain totally motionless, no sleep deprivation, just freedom to find the best balance of contemplative practice and action. Monks of old used a similar schedule. Their day was to get up, get food, go sit in the forest for the day, then come up for air in the late afternoon, so I hoped my plan was intense enough to get the job done even though I wasn't totally sure what the job might be.

I unpacked my gear for the retreat and went to bed but not to sleep. After dark the songbirds gave way to owls and lightning bugs and a bellowing chorus of frogs. By midnight it was all silent except crickets. Then something went rattling through the palmettos. It sounded huge like a deer or bear but I couldn't see anything in the darkness. It passed under a low branch and back out so it had to be small, maybe a coon or a possum or armadillo. The moon suddenly broke through the clouds and the raccoon came into plain view.

All the mental monsters I had created dissolved, and I walked into the front field in the blazing moonlight. The light in the pine field was so white it seemed like milky water pouring down out of the sky. A narrow waterfall of moonlight seemed to pour down in front of one tree. I sneezed, the noise flushed a heron and a huge black bird silhouette sailed croaking across the face of the full moon. The swamp roared with cicadas.

With no artificial light, nighttime had the most potential for the brain to switch gears into altered mental states. The brain hangs between sleep and waking and sensory deprivation is at max. I was able to maintain a total focus on the breath for a long time in the dark without falling asleep. That kind of focus on the breath really did stop verbal thought, and allowed a different form of consciousness to arise, first with thinking in pictures then with deeper shifts in awareness. If I could maintain that level of focus more consistently, sooner or later it would be a gateway into the more intense and in depth transcendent states of mind. Meditation and solitude were changing how the brain functioned, and going to the forest cultivated that shift even though it didn't seem like much was happening while I was just sitting under a tree.

Solitude works because we are a social species. Take away human friends and family and we make friends with the trees and birds and frogs and then we are part of that world and then the sense of self and other drops away. Later that night there was no name for the sentient energy that was suddenly shining through the form of the massive oak branches above the tent. Tree consciousness had no verbal ego-based component as human consciousness does so I couldn't experience trees from that kind of mind. Unlike raccoons, there was no shared easily recognizable mammalian body language, either. Nevertheless, an underlying consciousness common to both trees and humans was there. Perceiving it in myself, I could perceive it in the trees as well. There was just experiencing it without labeling it. That nonverbal not-naming mind was what allowed it to be experienced in the first place and it was somehow transcendent and sacred.

The more time I spent in the forest and at sea, the more I experienced reality as a pantheistic sentient universe in which consciousness exists in both material and nonmaterial states. Animism, the worship of nature spirits, is probably the most ancient form of human religion. Despite being routinely described as a "primitive belief system" by scholars, it might be more deserving of serious attention. When living in the natural world that is so full of living sentient beings all going about their own affairs, one spontaneously begins to experience not only the aliveness of all things but also the underlying source of that aliveness. Hunter gatherers' descriptions of spirit animating everything is simply an expression of that very real awareness.

In the modern world we systematically remove from our space almost all non-human life except for a few pets and house plants. We live in a dead indoor setting most of the time so it is easy to lose touch with that awareness of life and of the consciousness that permeates all things and is who we are. Then we dismiss the expression of this awareness by hunter-gatherers who do know it because their material technology is simple. After spending enough time alone in a forest, however, it becomes apparent that their description is dead-on accurate. That Zen vow about saving all sentient beings began to take on a whole new non-literal meaning.

Common enough to have names, these experiences of aliveness and inward energy in seemingly unaware things are called hierophanies (Gr: manifestation of the sacred) in western religion and savikalpa samadhi in Hindu philosophy. A person experiences the underlying unity of all seemingly distinct objects and feels themselves to be a part of it all. Separateness becomes an illusion as one experiences the aliveness of all things and the harmony that holds them together into a conscious whole. Perceiving something to be beautiful is a faint perception of this interbeing.

First-person accounts from all cultures and centuries describe these altered mental states that seem to be beyond life and death to the individual experiencing them. These descriptions are consistent enough to be considered reproducible by highly trained and committed practioners. Many mystical religious traditions have developed reliable methods for experiencing this wholeness and meaning in life.

In the Zen meditation tradition, this experience is especially emphasized and valued. The experience cannot be known rationally and is both beyond and encompassing individual consciousness. It can sometimes be reached in meditation or prayer. If practiced intensely, meditation can sometimes access certain extraordinary states of awareness that transcend birth and death. Isolation and alienation become deeply false states of mind since we are not separate from this universe that is alive, compassionate and responsive. We can then live in a spontaneously compassionate way.

Western mystics from the ancient Greek philosopher Plotinus to St. Augustine in Roman times to the Dominican Meister Eckhart of the 13th century to modern writers describe similar experiences. St. Teresa of Avila described a sudden illumination from within, rising up like a spring of great joy, St. Ignatius of Loyola perceived this reality with such clarity that everything seemed utterly new to him. He reported more comprehension in that moment than in all else he ever learned. To St. John of the Cross, transcendent awareness was not dependent on rational thinking ability but is a different instinctive part of the human mind, an alternate form of knowing. The Lutheran Jacob Boehme in the 17th century, gazing at sunlight reflecting off polished metal, suddenly entered into an altered state of mind. Going outdoors, he then perceived the aliveness in all things, and called it the experience of God in grass and plants. The 19th century poet Alfred Lord Tennyson often experienced a state in which his individuality became boundless being without a loss of ego based identity but with a clear and sure mind. Death is impossible, he said. It was not extinction but the only true life and he had total conviction as to the reality of the experience.

John Muir, wandering in the North American wilderness, perceived life in the ice and rocks. Nobelist writer John Steinbeck found it in the Sea of Cortez. After the intense work and danger of being on the moon and then returning to the orbiting spacecraft, Apollo 14 astronaut and astrophysicist Edgar Mitchell also had such an experience. He finally had time to rest on his way home from the moon. In that extraordinary setting between the earth and the moon, with 10 times more stars than are visible on earth, he suddenly became part of something huge and alive, experienced a sense of total harmonious connection of himself to all those celestial bodies.

Mystics directly experience and affirm an underlying unity in diversity. Theirs is the experiential first hand awareness of a form of mind that transcends the familiar brain based ego identity. A core insight of spiritual awareness, reported by mystics again and again, is that the universe is aware, sentient and creative and that we are not separate from that self-assembling and sentient process. Some universal consciousness, called Ground Consciousness, Original Face, or God by different religions, shapes itself into individual consciousness as a brain develops and then reverts back into a larger transcendent state when the material body dies. In this model the universe is not a collection of dead things. It is a single creative living event and we are an intrinsic part of it.

This perception may arise spontaneously but it can also be cultivated. One of the founders of the Zen tradition, Dogen, a Japanese monk in the 13th century, said "Cease to practice based on intellectual understanding, pursuing words and following after speech, and learn the backward step that turns your light inward to illuminate yourself. Body and mind of themselves will drop away and your original face will be manifest."

This state of mind is not just an isolated experience or ritual or prayer, it is openness and responsiveness to what is required of us at every given moment. A seed germinates and pops out of the ground on its own but only after it has first received good soil, water and nutrients. We ourselves are the good soil, while spiritual training provides the water and the nutrients.

Although neuroscientists are demonstrating that these events are associated with the brain's neural circuitry, those who experience such extraordinary states of consciousness uniformly insist that they provide a convincing sense of transcending life and death of the physical brain. The existence of such mental states suggests that the consciousness that comes from within the brain and dies when the brain dies may be only a part of the story.

Transcendental Monism is the philosophical argument that consciousness is primary and creates matter. There is one consciousness, we all participate in it, and the separateness that we feel is an illusion. In Buddhist philosophy this point of view is expressed as "form is emptiness and emptiness is form." When the still-before-thinking mind, the mind that is between thoughts and between breaths, becomes apparent, the experience may surface. It then becomes apparent that each individual human mind is part of the entire sentient universe, that there is no life and death, that nothing comes and goes, that everything in the universe is one thing.

It's not a matter of all or none, nor is it a you've finally got it sort of thing. Moments of altered perception arise from time to time but afterward one usually reverts back to a solitary ego based state. Having tasted it, however, we keep practicing to cultivate that state of mind so that it can become ever more present. The constant assurance of those who have walked this path is that we can personally experience this reality in ways that eliminate any personal doubt as to its reality.

At dawn, I went to a wildflower meadow to watch the sun break through the clouds. The color of a dawn actually peaks in intensity about halfway between darkness and sunrise. After that midway point, the colors fade to pastels until the sun comes up. A human life is like that, too. The most intense part of it is usually midway through when we are most fully engaged in the affairs of living. As we age, we also slow down, fading into pastel shades. Our lives then give way to a different reality that begins in that moment of transition known as death - or is it sunrise?

The ground beneath the longleaf pines was a carpet of blooming purple deer tongue and yellow goldenrod that was full of butterflies. A dozen wild turkeys ran across the field and disappeared under the big trees. Several deer watched me watching them as I sat motionless. We all stared at each other with enormous intensity. I instinctively settled into the hard wired steady gaze of a predator watching prey. The deer knew that and remained wary even though they were a long way off.

As I sat under trees with sunlight flashing through dark-green needles of cedar, cypress and pines, a strong east wind rattled the palm fronds, the nearby ocean was high and rough, and the season's last orange and yellow butterflies danced over the wildflowers. The earth, the wind and the waves were the ancient elements of earth, air and water. The fourth element, fire, was the sunlight flashing through the needles, powering the wind and ocean currents, and creating life as it did so.

The ancient elements move at different speeds. Air and water are always swirling and spinning rapidly in loops and eddies from the heat of the sun. Wind and rain become the swirling of ocean and atmosphere. The earth element drifts imperceptibly slowly, driven by its own internal heat in the super slow motion swirl of mountains rising and sediments eroding away, rocks forming and continents drifting over millions of years.

Compared to the movements of earth, air and water, butterflies, birds, humans and all living beings are a frenetic spinning of feeding, breathing, reproducing, perceiving, reacting, and endlessly cycling through life and death in a high-speed blur. Living beings are consciously aware of their environment in a way that rocks, wind, and water are assumed not to be. Life was present in that moment in the form of butterflies and also in the musical notes of a wind chime hanging on a tree which had come from the action of my conscious human mind.

Life exists at two levels: individuals by the millions flash on and off, on and off like fireflies in the night but at a larger level, life is one of the most powerful forces on earth. It has profoundly shaped the planet for millions of years and is almost equal in power to the other basic forces. From this perspective, a butterfly is as powerful as a mountain, containing all of life in its small vast self. An aware human being shares that power. In experiencing this connection, you receive a gift with no giver. But who is receiving what? The mountain, the butterfly, the human – are they the same or are they different?

According to many religious mystics and a few philosophers, consciousness may be a sixth basic force. We don't usually perceive it as one of the basic forces of the universe because it is not material. We can study earth, air, fire, water and life or, in scientific terms, matter and energy, and come to some understanding of their mechanisms, but nonmaterial consciousness has always been beyond our ability to measure in a laboratory.

Current brain imaging techniques are only now cracking open that door from a scientific perspective. From neurobiology it is increasingly clear that most of the day-to-day personality is a function of brain activity, levels of neurotransmitters, etc. Sensory perception, verbal thought, emotion, memory, dreaming are generated by the brain which then combines them into a "self" and gets attached to the existence of that self and fears its dissolution.

The sense of self, that which we call "I", is an amalgamation of the body, thoughts, and emotions, sensory experience, memories, desires and will. We normally equate our sense of self with the flux of conceptual thoughts and emotions in our brains. I think therefore I am. I feel, therefore I am. Words and memories create it anew in each moment. Memory is the glue that consolidates them into a discreet thing that has existed, exists now, is expected to continue on into the future and will persist throughout a lifetime. Those thoughts may be opinions, speculations, plans for the future, memories of the past but they are all passing thoughts, changing moment to moment.

So many thoughts in life begin with "I am" "I have" '"I want" "I like" "I don't like." We define and construct the individual sense of self with all these "I am" statements but they are all just thinking that we build up and modify every day. While functional thinking about dealing with a situation at hand is necessary, editorializing thinking, particularly opinions about what we dislike, just creates suffering. In long-term meditation, we see this and explore how it is affecting life day by day. What is underneath these "I am" mental habits? Only ask "what am I?" or "what is happening, what is this?" until the asking becomes a new mental habit. Don't worry about finding an answer that will settle the matter. It's actually asking "what is going on in this moment?" so the question is always new.

For years, I'd asked myself what's the point? What am I? What is consciousness? But there are problems with all these questions. "What's the point?" is vague and assumes that there is a point. It was rather like asking what is the point of continental drift. It's just the way the system works. It's simple but we want it to be more than that. "What am I?" is a little more precise. If we ask it long enough, it becomes a technique for letting go of I and thereby discovering the answer to the question. When I is dropped, then the question is better defined as "What is consciousness?"

Consciousness generally refers to humans and a very few other large brained species that have shown evidence of self-awareness, yet tiny jellyfish with only a few neurons can stalk and capture prey, avoid dangerous obstacles and apparently sleep on the sea floor. We cannot even imagine the mental state of a brittle star which perceives light with the crystalline structure of its skeleton or that of South American or African knife fish that use electric fields to signal to each other. There is neural activity at some level in all these creatures but the different brains that give rise to mental awareness, be they human, cat, crab or any of millions of other species, means that there are huge fundamental differences in the nature of the mental awareness of each species. Squid, jellyfish, starfish unlike anything on land are each as different from each other as they all are from a human being.

Humans will probably never know what these other beings experience due to our utterly different senses and nervous systems. The broader term sentient beings includes not only human mind but all those bizarre otherworldly creatures doing what they do, all those central nervous systems and sensory systems so totally different from our own, all those utterly incomprehensible processes of life in other phyla. The endless varied forms of sentience swarming at the bottom of the sea or of birds migrating, let alone of a plant, are just as integral to life on earth as is human consciousness.

Human consciousness is just one component of something much bigger and more varied than we can at this point even imagine. Humans are localized bundles of consciousness in a universe full of sentient beings that are infinitely creative and abundant. Sentience is pervasive throughout the living world, arising over and over again throughout the process of the evolution of living matter. Evolution, both cosmic and biological, is neither blind random chance nor deterministic and going inexorably toward some predetermined outcome. Rather it is an emergent spontaneous creative process of generating order and endless variation on themes. Matter self organizes into sentient life and life eventually produces species with self-aware consciousness. Is sentience a fundamental property of the universe? Is the universe itself aware? Might it follow a biological model of birth, reproduction and death? Is such an awareness one definition of God?

I didn't have answers to any of those big questions as I sat against a pine tree with frogs, crickets and the wind in full hullabaloo. A noisy ultra-lite plane passed slowly overhead. The racket seemed to tear a rip in the fabric of the place that slowly closed again as the plane passed. Or maybe I was the only one distracted by it. Maybe it takes a human to be bothered by human affairs. A hound bayed, running a deer out of season. The sound came closer and then the deer flashed past as it dove into a swamp. The hound lost the scent and quit baying. Most wild predators work by stealth and wolves hunt in packs. A solitary yelping hound is a human creation. The dog would have to leave the forest and find its human owner or starve. It was not part of the forest and the forest would not sustain it.

The dancing flashing of leaves and sunlight, the sound of wind, crickets and birds, the color and constantly changing sunlight and shadow, the intense life energy flowed like an ocean. Whatever was happening in this piece of pine forest with its sunlight and insects, its fox squirrels and flowers was what this planet has always been about. The natural world gives the exact same teaching day after day until we finally notice it. It takes a long time sitting to get to know a place, a long time to gain insight, a long time to find an answer to hardly spoken questions.

Sitting on a log as the proverbial bump, there was no attainment and nothing to attain in doing this. I would eventually leave the forest as empty-handed as I had arrived. It was just a matter of taking a treatment, of letting the impersonal serenity and effortlessness of nature infiltrate and permeate the mind until there was no longer a personal self apart from everything else observing anything.

An endless shower of pine needles fell silently, one here, one there. Small songbirds scuttered across the clear blue sunny sky in flocks like leaves before the wind. The sound of a distant highway penetrated until the wind rose a little so that the sound of the trees wrapped the forest back into its own reality, expelling the machine sound. The sense of wilderness appeared and disappeared here moment by moment with the wind.

Later that night bright moonlight, lightning bugs and chuck wills widows called across the landscape. I suddenly woke up and experienced my body as a dead corpse of guts, lifeless eyes, and dead muscles, like somebody else might discover it in a day or so. There was no suffering in it. The decaying of the body did not disturb conscious awareness at all. A few hours later, another of the odd images of the night appeared, this one of a disembodied consciousness with no identity labels and no emotion, dispassionately observing a cemetery from a hundred or so feet above the ground. There was no particular attachment to the place, just looking at it, moving slightly, seeing it from slightly different angles. That consciousness was impersonal and nonverbal, containing no thoughts, no words and no emotional content, only open ended observation. It was hugely different from the normal embodied human consciousness that consists of verbal thought and emotion and of the concept of a separate individual self. An impulse arose to go close enough to see a family name on a tombstone but nothing happened. This wasn't a lucid dream to be directed; it seemed to be a direct experience of consciousness after death, perhaps a memory or a prescient vision of a funeral. Then an odd sensation of a normally running brain suddenly seizing, stopping, missing a beat, freezing up arose. It happened repeatedly and it was frightening. Could it be a stroke? All at once, Anne was back, wide awake and more attached than ever to staying in this reality.

Insofar as Zen meditation practice is based on observation and experience rather than dogma, it resembles science. Unlike science, however, Zen considers subjective experience to be a valid source of insight once we are able to let go of the self- serving games of the ego and its endless desires. Also unlike science-based materialism, it does not limit consciousness to the brain or assume that death is the end of existence.

When a human body dies, the experiencing of a specific life in a given place and a specific time, with a specific name, social relationships, interests, aspirations and griefs ends. The personality defined by the body, including its gender, age, race, language, personal history of success and failure, must also cease when the body dies since gender, age, race, language, locality etc. all depend on this body. Disease often causes that personality to dissolve in the course of dying. We can watch it begin to dissolve when injury, strokes or dementia damage the physical brain. The elderly slowly let go of their lives, first involuntarily as they lose work, then mobility and health. Eventually many also let go of their individual personality as the brain ages and memory fails.

Many people equate Buddhism with materialistic philosophy because it doesn't speak explicitly of God or an eternal soul but, unlike scientific materialism, Buddhist philosophy doesn't claim that we completely cease to exist at the death of the brain. It affirms the survival and rebirth of some aspects of consciousness. In the Heart Sutra's "no old age and death and also no extinction of them," it explicitly points to survival of something although not exactly our current ego-oriented personal identity.

From neurobiology it is increasingly clear that most of the day-to-day personality is a function of brain activity, levels of neurotransmitters, etc. Sensory perception, verbal thought, emotion, memory, dreaming are generated by the brain which then combines them into a "self" and gets attached to the existence of that self and fears its dissolution.

Most scientists assert that since the evidence for non-brain based consciousness is not yet generally accepted by a majority of scientists, and since a lot of the individual personality is now demonstrated to be brain based, non-material consciousness doesn't exist and all consciousness disappears at the death of the brain. Yet there is rational evidence that some form of consciousness can survive the death of the physical brain, enough to provide hope if not certainty. Rebirth is not widely believed in the west but research on small children's accurate memories of a previous life suggests that it needs to be taken seriously.

Dr. Ian Stevenson and his successors at the University of Virginia have documented the accuracy of past life memories of some small children. This research has been successfully repeated by other investigators and is particularly hard to dismiss as wishful thinking or fantasy.

In addition to small children's accurate past life memories, the published observations of hospice nurses make it clear that mind can sometimes accurately see the future when close to death. The ability has been documented in people of many different cultures. And many records of out of body experiences associated with near death experiences include factual observations and knowledge subsequently shown to be accurate for which there is no rational explanation.

The usual rationalizations for why these experiences are not real have been disproved in a number of cases in which the individual was being monitored medically. Metabolic malfunctions in the brain generally lead to confusion, irritability, fear and belligerence. These are not reported with NDEs. On the contrary, thinking is enhanced, sharper and more alert than normal. It's not due to an oxygen starved brain or elevated levels of carbon dioxide. NDEs have occurred in surgical settings where these blood gases were being monitored and were at normal levels. Oxygen deprivation or an epileptic fit creates confusion that would preclude the complex coherent conversations that are reported. And these experiences occur in car accidents where there is no oxygen deprivation. A hallucinating person cannot leave and return to the hallucination at will but many dying people who claim to be conversing with unseen relatives are able to do precisely that. It's not a delusion of a dying brain since unconsciousness occurs within seconds of a heart stopping, and with no functional memory, the commonly reported lucid narratives would be impossible. Neither can they be attributed to the use of morphine since morphine produces a fragmented confused state of mind. Patients under inadequate anesthesia typically experience great pain while NDEs are pain free. If these experiences were fantasy, they ought to be highly variable as in dreams but they are remarkable consistent across different centuries and different cultures. If they were due to a release of endorphins, the experience should persist for a longer period of time than NDEs typically do. Most importantly, and unlike the commonly suggested pathologies, NDEs often lead to positive transformations in outlook on life, increased focus on living in the present and compassion. An NDE, like an Enlightenment experience, is one of the most profoundly meaningful and transformative human experiences possible.

Many skeptics dismiss qualitative evidence such as Stevenson's case histories or NDEs that resulted in accurate knowledge that would be impossible in a semiconscious person as "merely anecdotal and not science." However, an anecdote is in fact a rare complex event in an uncontrolled setting that cannot be easily reproduced. Being rare does not equal being false in every case nor does it justify dogmatically dismissing as lies or delusions the careful reports of credible witnesses. Careful descriptions of rare events sometimes point to areas where our current theoretical models are incomplete. Medicine and psychology are fields that originated with anecdotal information which are called case histories.

No matter how carefully this research is done, however, it is generally ignored by most other scientists. When asked about parapsychology as a field of research, philosophical materialists generally deny that there is any rational evidence at all and are often unaware of the substantial evidence that has been published in peer reviewed journals or the experimental rigor that is now used in the field. When asked what would be acceptable evidence, a level of stringent proof is often demanded that is far beyond what is required in other less philosophically controversial fields of research. Some retreat to a dogmatic statement that non material mind is impossible and that is that, at which point it isn't a hypothesis anymore, it is an ideology.

The majority of theologians also ignores or ridicules parapsychology because religion is based on faith. Even though there is evidence to support the theological belief in immaterial consciousness, depending on facts might later undermine other equally important beliefs such as the supremacy of one's faith above others or that personal salvation depends on accepting certain theological allegations as fact.

Before dogmatically denying any possibility of non-material mind or the survival of some form of consciousness after death, honest investigation requires that one review the substantial body of information that is available on the subject. Controversial information reported by professional scientists should not all be instantly dismissed simply because it doesn't fit the dominant theoretical paradigm. Our grasp of reality may remain incomplete until it expands beyond a strictly materialistic philosophy into one that can encompass transpersonal consciousness but we currently lack the technology to achieve that.

Because science says matter is paramount and religion says mind is, beliefs about the nature of reality are inconsistent, full of ignored paradoxes and shaky at their foundations, according to philosopher David Chalmers. Scientism, using science as a materialistic philosophy, to assert a totally reductionist scientific view that ignores and or denies subjective consciousness, simply cannot work, says Chalmers.

Although materialistic neurobiologists have generally declared consciousness to be a mere byproduct of brain complexity, as the iridescent color of a comb jellyfish is a byproduct of its feeding, we need to take it more seriously, he asserts. We are surer of the existence of consciousness than of anything else in the world. Consciousness is the most familiar thing and the most mysterious thing, the most vivid and the most diaphanous. The subject is at the intersection of science, philosophy and religion.

Developments first in physics and then in mathematics in the 20th century suggest that consciousness might be far more relevant to comprehending reality than had been previously assumed. The well-known double slit experiment in quantum physics showed that the presence of a conscious observer could somehow affect the behavior of photons. Biologists (and virtually everybody else) have considered quantum events irrelevant to the macroscopic everyday world, but current research strongly suggests that both photosynthesis and magnetic orientation in animals involve quantum effects, bringing the poorly understood realm of quantum physics into everyday macroscopic reality where its discovery that consciousness can affect the material world cannot easily be ignored.

Chalmers considers consciousness to be the largest outstanding obstacle in the quest for a scientific understanding of the universe. It is a natural phenomenon that arises in humans and in many other species, and there will prove to be natural laws that will explain it. Dualism is the philosophical assertion that mind and matter both exist. Religious belief in a soul that leaves the body at death is a form of dualism. Though this philosophical position has been out of scientific favor for centuries, Chalmers advocates a form of philosophical dualism in which everything remains a consequence of natural law and science is still intact but which also accommodates conscious transcendent experience. He makes the case that materialism is a philosophical argument not a scientific fact, that other philosophical positions are rationally defensible, that there is a credible body of data on human consciousness that materialism cannot explain and that science does not depend on materialism to succeed. He suggests the possibility that consciousness may turn out to be one of the fundamental forces of nature, not derived from physical systems and not derived from the four other known fundamental forces of physics. There is no information as yet on how a non-material form of consciousness could interact with the brain, but the risk in science is that of arrogance – to think that because we know so much that we must know more than we in fact do or that because some observation does not fit a current paradigm, that it must be invalid rather than pointing to a new area to investigate.

The brain's combination of reflections and memories is what we call I or me but in fact each of our brains is part of a vast ancient process of life arising from matter over and over. It has taken a long time for the universe to produce life and another long time for life to produce a self-aware species. Just as time is a conceptual invention that we lay onto a timeless cyclic alternation of light and dark, cold and hot, rainy and dry, so the sense of a separate unique identity is a conceptual invention that we lay on the endless cyclic process of cell fertilization, growth of a brain, and the firing of its neural networks with its tiny differences from one such cycling to another. The brain isn't "mine." It just makes the idea of "mine."

Why is it necessary to go through all this? What is the meaning of such a cycle in which we are all embedded? Is there is some larger scale function and meaning to consciousness beyond individual lifetimes? Either life has some ultimate meaning and purpose in the sense that we understand meaning and purpose or it does not. If it does not then all the time and effort trying to discover it in philosophy and religion is a waste of effort and there is no point in doing it at all. If it does have some meaning and purpose, then perhaps we'll discover it at some other point in such a transcendent life cycle and perhaps there is some reason for why we don't know what it is in daily life. It may be like asking what is the point of the fact that flowering plants reproduce with seeds and flowers instead of some other way. We haven't a clue as to why life is structured the way it is. There may be no special point beyond the fact that that is the way it evolved. Or there may be a point that we have no way of conceiving or comprehending.

The human mind is compelled to find or create patterns. Is this just a quirk of evolution or is that tendency itself part of some larger pattern? Are there patterns from somewhere else that unfold and govern a lifetime or is it all a meaningless random walk? These alternatives are always presented as an either/or, as omnipotent God's plan governing every little detail versus a meaningless flux, but maybe it's both. Maybe there is some theme and higher purpose playing out but doing so in the midst of a lot of random haphazard noise. Maybe this and maybe that. Maybe we should sit down, be quiet and see what appears. This point where science has reached its current frontier is precisely the point at which Zen practice begins.

SEASONS OF THE SEA

The planet swarms and dances with life,
in a multiplicity of forms that are nearly
unknown on dry land. ...An aquarium lays
out the graceful and the bizarre, presents
us with the ultimate Zen kong an of
biological form and diversity, leaves us to
wonder "What is this? What on earth does
it really mean? How does it come to be?"
and also like a Zen kong an, leaves us to
find that answer on our own.

It was a quiet Friday afternoon with nothing much happening when suddenly the door burst open.

"Hurry up," yelled a neighbor, "there's a baby porpoise stranded at the boat ramp."

I'd just been wishing something would happen — it apparently had. Jack and I raced over the back roads to the landing, and there she was — a 4-foot-long baby porpoise in three inches of water in the marsh grass. She seemed healthy enough as she called with high-pitched whistles. The fisherman who had first noticed her poured water over her back to keep her wet. We had permits to handle endangered sea turtles, but not marine mammals. If we carried her to one of our aquarium's sea-water tanks, we'd be breaking the law and if she died, we'd be in no end of trouble. But when whales strand, pulling them back into deeper water usually doesn't work either. There was no adult porpoise anywhere around and a solitary baby, if it didn't become a snack for the first shark it ran into, would starve to death. It probably beached itself instinctively to avoid danger.

While the fisherman stood watch, my husband and I went racing back to the office and hit the phone. Amazingly, we caught the right people in time and got official clearance to bring the little porpoise into shelter while they called a crew from a larger aquarium several hundred miles away to come and get her. They had bigger saltwater tanks than we did, tanks that could hold her along with other porpoises.

We went back with a bedspread and used it as a sling to carry her to our place. The biggest tank was about 4 feet deep and 20 feet in diameter. And full of blue crabs. By this time a half dozen adults and kids had appeared, and they grabbed nets and moved the pinching crabs to another tank while we held the frightened little orphan in her sling against the side of the tank. When we let her go, she panicked, throwing water all over us as she tried to find safety. After a few seconds, she calmed down and moved more slowly around the tank. She was crying frantically like any baby that had lost its mother and was scared to death.

The pickup team wouldn't arrive before 10 p.m. and someone had to stay with her constantly to ensure she didn't get hurt somehow. That turned out to be no problem as more and more people in town heard what was happening and came to watch. As she circled the small tank, everybody rubbed her back. As the evening passed, she settled down, always staying close to somebody. The physical contact seemed to reassure her. If people moved away from the tank she would become frightened again. It was like taking care of a little child.

When the people came to get her, they said she was only a few days old. They would get her used to a bottle at first and then try to put her in with a female porpoise as a foster mother. Not any porpoise would do. They had to locate one with an easy-going temperament that would accept a strange baby. And she had to be trained to come to a bottle in case the foster mother didn't have enough milk.

Several months later, a few wild porpoises still patrolled the beaches as summer turned to fall. That year's marine biology class walked along the shore, all of us bundled up against a cold north wind that was blowing with bared fangs across the bay. The first winter cold front had swept through the night before and the sky looked like a blue porcelain dish above our heads. The full-moon tide had fallen hard and fast that morning, pushed by both gravity and the wind and the tide flats were dry for a quarter of a mile off the beach.

The beach we walked on, I explained, was a tiny piece of the 2700 mile long beach that extends from New England to Texas. Composed of almost 300 barrier islands as well as long stretches of barrier beach shorelines, they are long narrow deposits of sand and shells built up by wind, waves and currents. The sand got there as sediments transported to the coast by Ice Age rivers when sea level was lower. As sea level has risen in the last 10-12,000 years, the sand deposits have been inundated, picked up by currents and reworked into our modern beaches and shores.

Of all marine environments, a beach is one of the most barren of marine habitats, with fewer species than almost any other ocean environment. But those species that do live there, hanging on in surging waves and moving up and down the beach with the tide, are some of the most specialized of all marine animals and don't usually occur elsewhere.

The constant shifting of the sand by waves, wind and current create an unstable surface in the surf zone. The marine animals that live there have bodies specially adapted for rapid digging. Mole crabs, which are about an inch long, have egg shaped smooth white bodies with legs that fold tightly under the streamlined body when they aren't digging into the sand.

And a beach is exposed to extremes of temperature. I found myself hurrying through the mini-lecture. It was just too cold to stand there in the wind for very long. Everybody was hunkered up and stamping their feet to stay warm. I waded into the surf, collected some mole crabs with a dip net and carried them back up the beach to the rest of the class even though normally everybody would have been wet and happy collecting the crabs themselves. The last time I'd brought a class here it had been August, around 100 degrees, and we had all dove into the water as soon as we arrived to avoid the oncoming heat stroke from the long hike through the dunes. Seasonal change was no abstract concept on this beach.

One relatively sheltered stretch of the shore was protected from the waves and had an exposed meadow of sea grass. Foot high yellow towers arose, scattered here and there across the green carpet, looking vaguely like castles. The boring sponges had bumps all over their surfaces and chimney like holes on the top of each cylindrical spire.

Sponges are among the most colorful animals of the sea. Some are orange or red, others may be yellow or lavender or white or even blue. The only multicellular animals with no nervous system, no muscles or other organs, sponges are a sort of living sieve, almost a consortium of individual self-sufficient cells. If shredded (not limb from limb but cell from cell) the cells swim about, refind each other and regroup themselves into a new sponge - a trick that's totally impossible for most organisms who have complex, elaborately organized bodies full of specialized tissues and organs that can't survive once their interactions are severed. They pump seawater through endless channels that penetrate throughout the sponge and filter microscopic food out of the water. And the channels are often full of worms and shrimps and crabs that live inside the sponge, collecting food from the water flow - like so many tenants inside a high rise condominium. Because of their simplicity, sponges are generally dismissed as the most primitive of multicellular forms, a failed attempt to build a complex animal. In terms of species number, however, they are as successful a group as the mammals. And on rocky areas of sea floor, they are often the dominant species, outcompeting vastly more complex animals.

Underneath the boring sponges, dozens of ruby red shrimp, each about an inch long, sheltered in an inch of water, waiting for the tide to return. Called red cleaners, they jump on fish and pick parasites or injured tissue off the host. Another tide flat along the shore of a nearby estuary was also exposed and it was covered with edible big white shrimp, hundreds of shrimp stranded by the unusually fast fall of the wind-driven tide as they had moved along the shore toward the Gulf of Mexico. These shrimp would not complete the fall migration from the marshes at the head of the bay to the open sea, but their misfortune was our gain. Everybody forgot about the cold weather. Scientific theory and learned discussion of marine animal migration was on hold as the students switched from ecology to fisheries biology, more specifically to harvesting the marine resource at our feet. Lunches were emptied out of ice chests and somebody took off to a convenience store across the bridge for more ice as everybody else slogged around in the mud picking up the shrimp. Marine biology was all well and good but this was dinner, this was real.

It isn't just birds or white shrimp that migrate in the fall. With a few cold fronts, the water chills, gets stirred up and choppy. It's a signal to all the crabs and fish and shrimp that the warm shallow food-rich inshore waters of summer are changing and will soon be too cold for survival. Just like birds headed south for the winter, they move offshore to deeper water, water that will stay relatively warm through the brief chill of a Gulf Coast winter.

It was also run season for mullet — the year's young fish formed schools and ran along shore, their bodies ripe with eggs and sperm, to spawn in deep open water. Their microscopic offspring would some-how ride the currents back into the bays and marshes a few months later in early spring. Kemp's ridley sea turtles disappeared from their crab rich grass-bed feeding grounds — some would move south, some would bury in the mud, hibernating like pond turtles till the water warmed up again.

In the surf zones of the Gulf Coast west to the Mississippi, mother electric rays that came inshore to birth their young in August and Sep-tember were headed back to offshore bars in 30 feet of water. The new-born brown spotted babies would stay on, feeding on tiny worms and burrowing sea anemones until January cold forced them to remain bur-ied and inactive until spring time. Horseshoe crabs would abandon the breeding beaches they'd visited every full and new moon all summer, not to return till March, leaving those beaches to migrating butterflies. Man-atees retreated from the coastal sea grass beds back to freshwater springs that have warm water year round. The microscopic floating plants that kept the waters murky but rich in food all summer would die off. The water would become crystal clear, but there'd be nothing to watch. Come the full moon in April everything would explode into life again. The seasons of the sea, as fishermen and marine biologists all know, are as sharply marked as those of the land.

After weeks of hard winter rains, the normally clear salt water in St Andrew Bay had been flooded out. When Doug Gleeson, a diver from the aquarium, and I pulled up to a boat ramp there a few days later, the water in the boat basin looked like a black water river or a cypress swamp. Visibility in the opaque black water was less than zero. We had planned to dive the rock jetties at the mouth of the bay for sea urchins but the diving conditions looked hopeless.

Built decades before to stabilize the navigation channel, the jetties accidently created a great artificial reef as well. In summer, the rocks provided habitat for multicolored tropical reef fish normally found only far offshore in the northern Gulf. Beaugregories and rainbow colored wrasses flashed their vivid yellow and sapphire, red and emerald green selves in and out of crevices in the rocks. Barracuda and amberjack patrolled the deeper edges. In the brief winter, spiny black sea urchins, red, brown and green seaweed gardens and vast schools of tiny transpar-ent baby fish had the chilly water mostly to themselves.

A northern cold water species growing on the jetties near the southern end of its geographic range, the urchins were only fertile during the winter months. When they were fertile, biology professors used their eggs to demonstrate cell fertilization and embryonic development in the classroom. It didn't look like we'd find much, but having driven a long way, we launched the boat and ran out to the main channel to have a look. And sure enough, as we left the lagoon the black water abruptly gave way to the usual green and blue sparkle of salt water. A wavy line marked the boundary between the two different worlds of swamp and ocean. The tide was nearly high and salty Gulf water had pushed the freshwater flood back up into the bay. The water over the jetties was clear and we could dive after all.

The wind was strong out of the southwest. On the opposite side of the channel, breakers raced up the other jetty and refracted across the channel. They came sweeping over the rocks on our side in cascades of sea foam. It was like surfing in scuba gear to make it from our anchorage over the top of the rocks to the outside of the jetty. Timing was critical. The swells were too strong for puny humans to resist. As each one came in, we hung onto a rock and then let the backwash carry us between the boulders. Like salmon going upstream, we wiggled and kicked until we were over the rocks and then dove twenty feet to the bottom, into the calmer water beneath the heaving surface.

As we swam along the base of the rocks, it was obvious that the black water had been here. The urchins, which are intolerant of low salinity, had been hit hard by the freshwater flood. Normally covering the rocks by the thousands where they graze on seaweed, the spines of the victims littered the sandy bottom. Some had not died and looked healthy as ever. What did they do differently, I wondered, from their less fortunate brethren?

Doug lost his weight belt and we returned to the boat. He took mine and went back to look for his, while I waited in the skiff. As he returned to the rocks, the tide began to fall. And as it did, a wall of black swamp water advanced down the channel, replacing the retreating salt water, headed inexorably towards the jetty. There was almost no mixing. A line of foam marked the boundary - one side was black, the other was clear. It passed the anchored boat and enveloped the rocks. The visibility was suddenly not quite zero, but the water was a dark reddish brown. Every day, it seemed, the urchins got a few hours of relief from the fresh water at high tide and then got nailed again when the tide turned.

A few minutes later Doug was back at the boat, still minus a weight belt.

"How'd this war of the waters look from below?" I asked.

"A reddish fog," he said. "It darkened and lightened with each swell that swept overhead. It was the weirdest thing I've ever seen in the water," he grinned. It made my day too. If we ever think we really know a place, we probably haven't looked enough.

Huge red winter jellyfish called *Rhopilema* were everywhere. Few life forms on earth are more different from the familiar fuzzy warm mammals of dry land than the jellyfish and their relatives. And at approximately 9000 species strong, they outnumber mammal species by almost 2 to 1. Few animals are more quickly dismissed as insignificant by humans than jellyfish. The very word is almost synonymous with primitive. Yet the coelenterates - the group of animals that includes jellyfish as well as their relatives the corals, sea anemones, and hydroids - represent 9000 different ways to make a living using the simple body design of the group, 9000 variations on an elegant theme. These so called primitive creatures invented the neuron, the same basic brain cell with which humans write and read books. They invented the contractile muscle cell that we still use to walk across the room. And this group invented warfare and offensive weapons. They aren't primitive, just cleanly designed. Their deadly stinging cells make them one of the few groups that can still hold the human super predator at bay - when jellyfish move in on swimming beaches around the world, we flee. The stinging cells are like microscopic harpoons with the barb and line coiled up in a pouch. The least touch triggers the harpoon, sending it flying into the flesh of its prey. All members of this group sting. The ones that we can handle safely simply have barbs that fail to penetrate our relatively thick skins.

These animals do all this with a body composed of only two layers of living cells with a gelatinous layer in between, and they come in two basic models. The swimming jellyfish or medusa has a mouth surrounded by stinging tentacles that hang head down as it pulses its way through the water. If this basic form is turned over so that the mouth and tentacles reach upward and the animal remains attached to the bottom, the sea anemone or polyp form results. If the body is built of thousands of tiny interconnected polyps to form a colony, we have all the many species of hydroids, soft corals and the stony corals that build spectacular reefs in tropical waters.

At the university where I taught, a seminar was underway the next day on jellyfish. As I came into the room and sat down, a young woman stood up and began her talk about jellyfish and other open-ocean animals that build transparent soft "jelly"-like bodies — who they are, what they eat, how they catch it, their impact on the world around them. The speaker was a graduate student and this was of one of a series of student talks on marine ecology.

The student focused her talk on what she had found in the library. The faculty members at the seminar led a discussion, intermingling knowledge from the published literature with their own personal experiences and insights The professor directing the group had been my major professor years before. The student ran some video footage of a salp, a creature with a more or less tadpole-shaped body that builds an envelope or house of jelly and then filters water through to capture microscopic food. An alien from space might look something like that, I mused, glittering, flashing, hanging suspended in space. What would it be like to live as one of these mid-water beings? A comb jelly, perhaps, floating, tentacles stretched out, waiting for some small creature to hit and be stuck then reeled in. Or one of the bioluminescent jellyfish in the blackness of the deep oceans. What is this universe that manifests itself in these eerie pulsing life forms anyway? WHAT ON EARTH IS THIS? In the Zen tradition, Great Question or Great Doubt is what motivates the spiritual quest and it had suddenly popped up again. All of our knowledge suddenly seemed like a tiny raft on a very big ocean indeed.

It was amazing — 18 people enthusiastically discussing the details of how a comb jelly traps its food, how it fits into the intricate web of interactions that make up this living planet. There aren't very many people who care enough about that sort of thing to devote a career to it. Universities provide a place where they can find each other.

Public aquariums are another place where people like this find each other. I had an appointment early one morning with a scientist at the New England Aquarium in Boston. When we finished our business, I walked back out into the huge central display area. The aquarium hadn't opened for the day but a new exhibit of cow nosed rays had just been

68

completed and the press was there for a sneak preview that would hope-fully get some visitor generating publicity.

About 30 people stood quietly around the huge shallow tank, eating bagels and muffins, half preoccupied with their own conversations and half watching the graceful soaring of several dozen rays as they circled and circled, slowly beating the tips of their flattened bodies, looking for all the world like kites come to life. As they passed, almost everybody reached out a hand to gently touch them or call them like a kitten. But they seemed unaware of anything other than their own slow flying real-ity.

Cutting through the soft murmur of conversation was an occasional shriek from the penguins in the adjacent large pool. Some stood on the artificial rock ledges and islands in their urban ocean while others floated at the surface, looking like ducks except that they paddled with their wings instead of their feet. They looked like birds in a way that evaporates when they stand upright. And when they dove they flew like falcons underwater, swerving and darting at high speed, until flight and swimming were one thing.

Sea turtles and sharks and tarpon and jacks, angelfish and mackerel swam endlessly in the 2 story tall circular center tank, moving forever in a counter clock wise waltz. They didn't seem to notice how the still-ness and the mystery of the place abruptly evaporated when the front doors opened and the first school field trip of the day poured in a flood through the entrance. Outside the big yellow buses were lined up 8 deep, waiting to unload. Where the adults had stood quietly in front of the ray exhibit, the kids squatted and jumped, running back and forth from one vantage point to the next. The air was solid with the loud shrieks and chatter of excited children who knew a good thing when they saw it.

It was easy to understand what these young fellow humans were thinking but the fish were tougher. Do fish think as they amble around? What would a fish think about anyway, what sort of fishy thoughts? What is the internal reality of a fish? Orthodox science emphatically asserts that they don't, that only a few big brained mammals have even the possibility of awareness but in fact we really haven't a clue one way or the other so why not wonder?

In smaller aquaria mounted in the walls rainbow colored small fish picked over their coral habitat, some looking for their own version of bagels and muffins, some just cruising about. One tank had 3000 schooling silver menhaden, each only a few inches long. Their silver fluid movement glittered and flashed. The tank was solid fish, and it was the ultimate abundance, life coalescing out of water with intensity beyond comprehension.

The planet swarms and dances with life, in a multiplicity of forms that are nearly unknown on dry land. The graphic displays on the walls of the aquarium explained what little we know about camouflage and schooling and warning coloration and all that sort of thing but they didn't come close to answering the real questions these living displays ask. An aquarium lays out the graceful and the bizarre, presents us with the ultimate Zen kong an of biological form and diversity, leaves us to wonder "What is this? What on earth does it really mean? How does it come to be?" and also like a Zen kong an, leaves us to find that answer on our own.

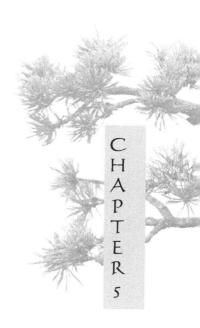

ECOLOGICAL MUSEUMS

To see all those eagles and owls sitting on sky nests lost in a sun and fog swept wilderness was an incredible experience, an assurance that this planet is still functional. But it was more. Flying with the eagles on a silver gleaming winter morning along a living coast was a spiritual gift of wholeness and beauty.

A bald eagle sitting on her nest looks like a hen sitting on hers. She sits in the same posture with the same total commitment to stillness, her mighty wings held low and spread a little to the side, protecting her eggs with her total being. Unlike chickens, however, she's sitting in a huge nest a hundred feet in the air, nestled in the crown of a big pine tree. The tree is lost in a forest that stretches unbroken for miles along a wilderness coast of marsh and sea and winter storm clouds racing ashore. Ducks by the thousands swim the marsh creeks and impoundments at her feet, insuring that her chicks will be well fed in a few months. At the brink of extinction only a few years ago because of human recklessness with pesticides, bald eagles have made a comeback.

One of the places critical to their recovery has been the St Marks National Wildlife Refuge which surrounded my retreat swamp. Its coastal wilderness and growing waterfowl population are eagle heaven. One of over 400 national wildlife refuges nationwide that protect over 150 million acres of land, St Marks, founded in 1931, includes about 65,000 acres. In addition to bald eagles, endangered wood storks, red cockaded woodpeckers and a few whooping cranes also call it home. The world's rarest sea turtle, the Kemp's ridley, is abundant. The endangered headliners flourish there because of the overall richness of the marsh, forest, cypress and sea grass ecosystems. Huge populations of shrimp, crabs, mullet, redfish and other marine species survive. Manatees cruise its coastal waters. Hundreds of thousands of migratory ducks and other water birds winter in the coastal impoundments. The hardwood swamps are rich in otters, wood ducks, swallow tailed kites and night herons. Deer, turkey and huge furry fox squirrels are common in the pine forests.

The refuge protects part of a 200 mile long publicly owned coastline, the Florida Big Bend. Some 36 species of endangered, threatened or otherwise protected wildlife flourish there. It's one of the last big pieces of mostly uninhabited coast left in the lower 48 states, and is a national leader in preserving the almost extinct long leaf pine ecosystem.

There's another difference between a nesting eagle and a chicken. To see the eagle, it takes a helicopter and a biologist who can locate the one tree out of thousands in that unbroken forest that she's in. The helicopter ride was one that refuge biologists make twice a year to census how many are nesting and how many young they produce annually. The most accurate and quickest way to do that is to travel the way the eagles do, see the world more or less as they see it.

I wrote a column in the local newspaper and I wanted to do an essay about the refuge and its eagles. The copter met us at the boat ramp parking lot by the pre-Civil War St Marks lighthouse. We lifted off and the first nest was only a few hundred feet away on a nearby marsh hammock. She was home. We quickly veered away to avoid disturbing her and headed east. Immediately another eagle passed us in midair, flying back towards the nest we had just left. The males and females trade off on nest duty, with one on the nest and the other out hunting. Eggs take about five weeks to hatch and then it's another ten to twelve weeks to fledging. At the next nest, the eagle flew, circling her nest, and we counted 1 egg.

We headed further east over the palm hammocks near the Aucilla River and swung back to pick up a nest we had missed. The refuge biologist had a map in his lap and the navigational coordinates of each known nest, but that only got us to the general vicinity. He seemed to know the location of every nest in the forest, pointing out the window across trees that looked indistinguishable from all the others to me but weren't to him.

"It's over in that direction at about 9 o'clock." And so it was. At 200 feet, the wilderness coast seemed to stretch on forever as it always has, untouched by humans and their bulldozers. Bare cypresses, maples and oaks formed a band of low swamp forest between the marshes and the green pines behind them. Off to the left the open Gulf gleamed silver and gold. On the hammocks in the marsh, the individual pines stood like toothpicks, open space around each one and we could see the forest as it truly was, an open savannah.

A solitary eagle sat in a tall pine but it wasn't on the nest.

"We picked up an injured eagle a few months ago near here - it might have been part of this pair," he commented. Eagles mate for life, returning each year to their own nest.

"There's the next one," he said, pointing casually out the window. The pilot circled left and I finally saw it. The bird hesitated and then flew. Two eggs in that nest. She quickly returned as we moved away.

"Next one will be on that larger hammock up ahead, at coordinates 30.0670 and 83.8932." She was. We swung up the Aucilla River, passing osprey nests and a flock of cormorants flying beneath us. The outboard motor eating limestone that is the bane of fishermen gleamed orange through the dark water as the river twisted and wound its way deep into the forest. We headed back west, inland from the marsh. The boundary between federal land and private paper company land was obvious -- on one side were tall pines and eagles, on the other side there were just plantations and the rutted muddy scars of a recent clear-cut.

The gusting wind swung the tail of the helicopter from side to side, making it difficult to get accurate navigational fixes. A nest had been reported in the area but we couldn't locate it. Finally we found a partial nest with a great horned owl instead of an eagle, its grey-brown plumage barely visible against the brown nest. Owls often occupy old eagle nests. As the national symbol of the United States, bald eagles have been the focus of long and mostly popular effort to save them from extinction. The only way to save the bird is to preserve its habitat and in doing that, we also save thousands of other species, like the great horned owl, that don't have the same political clout.

Coming back out over the St Marks River, we overflew the remains of the 17th century Spanish fort. Just upriver was the next nest. The eagle was home, sitting on three eggs. The nest near Wakulla Beach had another owl and one in a huge old cypress tree had an eagle. Then another owl and then an eagle. As we flew, the foggy scudding cloud ceiling lowered and lowered, stormy weather pulled in off the Gulf by an approaching cold front. One more nest and the eagle was home there too. Finally we had to turn back. Every nest we'd checked had a bird. To see all those eagles and owls sitting on sky nests lost in a sun and fog swept wilderness was an incredible experience, an assurance that this planet is still functional. But it was more. Flying with the eagles on a silver gleaming winter morning along a living coast was a spiritual gift of wholeness and beauty.

The eagles were there because of the green and brown intertidal salt marshes that stretched for miles along the coast. The vast expanse of shallow ocean seaward of the shore prevents large waves from forming so that the water flows quietly in and out of the marsh with no surf. Large river systems that could supply beach sand to that coast do not exist so in addition to having no wave action to build beaches, there is very little sand with which to build them.

To the west, the broad shallow offshore bottoms give way to deeper water next to shore. This allows the wind to build the waves that endlessly wash ashore. The waves carry sand brought to the coast by big rivers over millions of years. Waves move the sand along the shore, piling it up in sand bars and beaches and preventing the growth of marsh plants along the open coast. The intertidal marsh coastline of the Big Bend is replaced with long white stretches of beach, dunes and barrier islands from the Ochlockonee to the Mississippi River.

Besides the east-west boundary between the marsh and beach shorelines, the northern Gulf coast is an approximate boundary between the temperate zone that stretches north along the Atlantic coast and the tropical oceans to the south. The plants and animals are a mixture of cold water loving species growing as far south as they can and tropical species from the Caribbean growing as far north as they can. In summer months, coral reef fish and invertebrates more typical of the Bahamas appear in some coastal areas only to disappear when winter arrives. They either die or move onto limestone outcrops in water deeper than 60 feet where the chill of a brief three month winter doesn't penetrate. Each spring the populations are renewed by microscopic young stages carried north on the Loop Current, a section of the oceanic Gulf Stream that pumps tropical water into the northern Gulf of Mexico at a rate of millions of cubic meters of water per second.

The day after the helicopter trip I was back out in the marsh, this time on foot. A salt marsh is a place of rigorous, sun-flattened, windswept simplicity. Only a few species of grasses dominate the land for miles. On the Atlantic coast, cord grass is dominant while needle rush is limited to the highest marsh next to the forest. On the Gulf coast, a vast expanse of brown needle rush sweeps across the land, with ribbons of green cord grass twisting through it along the banks of the salt creeks. Up close, the brown dissolves into a mixture of dark green living reeds and white woody dead ones. Red and green patches of two species of succulents grow on the white sand of bare salt flats next to the forest. Patches of spike grass grow between the open flats and the edges of the needle rush, their angled slender leaves providing visual relief from the spare vertical lines of the other plants. Each vegetation type, each color reflects subtle changes in elevation of this seemingly flat land, changes so small the eye can't detect them but big enough to make a difference in how many hours of the day the tide covers a given area. As the tide began to move back in, sliding silently, almost imperceptibly up the creek, its movement was revealed only by bubbles on the surface, shining silver against the exposed black mud banks. In salt marshes, the sea penetrates the land like a lover, gently and slowly, not crashing against it in attack as it does on beaches and rocks.

Rain fell for an hour and when it slowed down fog appeared against the forest wall. I couldn't tell if it was blowing in on the wind or coalescing on the spot. The great blue herons and snowy egrets sat hunched in the rain along the banks of the creeks. They could only sit, waiting for the wind to shift, the tide to fall, the water to be lower. In time it would. Some lines from a Zen poem came to mind: "Beyond the door is the land of stillness and light. Spring comes, the grass grows by itself."

Five or six periwinkle snails were piled in a heap at the base of each blade of grass. The plants would be a refuge, a tower of escape they would climb as the rising tide brought with it shell-crushing, hungry blue crabs. By high tide the grass would appear to support a crop of white berries. A few fiddler crabs wandered through the fat red saltworts on the open sand flat — that seemed to be all. But there was an incredible abundance of young crabs, shrimp, fish — the year's crop of marine life — growing in the murky creeks. The animals of the marsh stayed mostly hidden. Tiny young fish and shrimp, crabs and snails, still too small to see, rode in on each turn of the tide. Without a net you'd never know it. The mammals moved in by night, and from the tracks, the nearby game trail was a regular raccoon highway.

Flock after flock of cormorants passed over, several hours late in the morning trek to their feeding grounds. The storm, it seemed, had delayed them just like any other commuters. At high tide in a storm, the tidal creeks were full and overflowing into the marsh. At low tide, the bare sand surface of the salt flats would be sculpted, textured like brocade, a fabric of white sand accentuated with coal black grain-sized bits of water-soaked wood. Bright little fiddler crabs endlessly rework the sand to harvest the microscopic plants that grow on the surfaces of individual sand grains. Scattered across the white and black land, glittering like diamonds in the sun, would be tiny clear grains of quartz crystal. But now, flooded, the pattern was erased, its makers sleeping buried below the surface until the next low tide. White sand, clear water, streaks of marsh grass and streaks of rain — each drop hit with a white flash of light and the water surface shimmered from the vibrations of impact after impact.

Suddenly, I realized that I was in too deep to go back, in too far to retreat from an alternative life style that had me standing in a remote marsh in the rain asking the universe to explain itself when everybody else was far away, earning a living, doing the business of the world. It was a scary moment. And yet, what a gift, this interplay of light and water bringing life as it penetrated the grassland.

There is a lot of land in the United States that's official, legal bureaucratic wilderness. And there is a lot more public land, hundreds of thousands of acres of it, that's more or less wild with native ecosystems in various stages of disarray or recovery from earlier disturbance. They are ecological museums, places where we can see a little bit of how the world used to look, places not quite in sync with the daily realities of modern life, places that are fundamentally irrelevant to most people who aren't biologists or nature lovers. These lands aren't irrelevant, though. If you take care of the habitat, the endangered species will often take care of themselves. And preserving them, preserving all the parts that make up this planet — not stealing the options of our children's children — is the most truly conservative approach in the long run. But taking care of the habitat requires a lot more than putting up a fence. It also means making sure the food chain isn't full of toxic waste and the rain isn't so acid that it kills aquatic life and forests.

Wilderness, real wilderness — places where human influences don't reach at all — is almost nonexistent. The deep open ocean is probably the closest thing to true wilderness left on Earth. Yet widespread over-fishing and the decimation of marine mammals and turtles have hit even those unexplored areas in ways we can't even fully describe. What is left is a series of those ecological museums, scraps of longleaf pine and tall grass prairie and rain forest and coral reef that barely hang on.

Inland from the refuge's marsh, a forest of majestic longleaf pines interspersed with cypress swamps stretched for miles. The towering straight trees grew in open groves, scattered across a meadow-like ground cover of grasses and herbaceous plants. Prior to European settlement, much of the southern United States was carpeted with those forests. The sunny open floor of the forest supported an endless array of wildflowers. The flowers gave Florida its name, la Florida, place of flowers.

Once dominating the coastal plain from North Carolina to Texas, this landscape has been nearly destroyed by farming, logging, and the suppression of fires. By the 1920s and '30s, the virgin forests were cut down and what survives today is young second-growth. Less than 2% of the original acreage survives as remnants in parks, private estates and national forests and wildlife refuges. Much of that is badly degraded from lack of the lightning-set fires that once swept the land every few years, removing competing hardwood species.

Over one hundred rare or endangered plants grow only in this eco-system. Many are endemic, occurring nowhere else. Animals of the longleaf include fox squirrels, red-cockaded woodpeckers, huge gopher tortoises, pine and indigo snakes. Graceful black-and-white wood storks once soared overhead going to their wetland feeding and roosting areas scattered over the landscape. Today virtually all of these animals are endangered, threatened or species of special concern. It's a simple rela-tionship – no fire, no longleaf. No longleaf, less species of plants and animals on earth.

A few federal and state parks still have bits of forest, but the largest surviving tracts on public land are on national forest, military bases and wildlife refuges like the one that surrounded my camp. To spend some time in these tiny remnant forests is to get a glimpse of the earlier wild landscape that once was. Lots of people wander in the wilderness and each brings a different set of ideas, values and so forth to the experi-ence. The mental baggage you carry influences what you see and how you understand it, but if you stop and still both the body and the mind, then the land itself becomes more apparent, the other face of the forest reveals itself. The things that are unnoticed when walking and talking — wind, insect song, small birds — become dominant. It is easier to engage the non-verbal forest with a quiet mind, but whether in a Zen retreat or a forest, shutting off the internal chatter, even for a minute, is a hard thing to do. Even when the mind does become quiet, it only stays that way for a few minutes before the speeches begin again.

Walking in one of the preserved remnants of the once vast longleaf forest on the refuge that surrounded my little piece of forest, I wondered if there would be more large vertebrates if this were a virgin forest that stretched for miles. Would I have a better chance to stalk a bear or a panther? Then I saw something a few hundred feet away on the branch of a pine sapling. Freezing, I first thought it was a rare fox squirrel but it was so absolutely unmoving for so long I convinced myself it was just a bend in the wood. Then tail fur moved in a breeze and I moved closer. Two or three times bigger than a grey squirrel with a black mask over its eyes, it dropped off the other side of its perch and discreetly walked away on the ground, its huge bushy tail arched behind it. The size of small cats, fox squirrels are too big to leap from branch to branch like grey squirrels. A pygmy rattlesnake was curled up asleep in a dead oak leaf.

In the ocean, population levels are much higher and the larger animals don't stay hidden, the little ones do. In the forest large vertebrates are scattered and hidden while insects are everywhere. In the forest, everything was alive and doing what it did effortlessly with no confusion as to why and how. While insects were the abundant animals visible on the ground, there was also a subdued quiet layer of bird song overhead in the branches. Plants and insects, bird song, wind, the hum of crickets and cicadas, an occasional buzz of other flying insects, the occasional bark of a tree frog after rain, these were the voice of the forest.

The last time I'd come to this spot had been just before sunset and the forest had been bathed in a glowing magical light. This time I arrived about an hour earlier and the light was transitional, not the flat color-bleached light of hot summer midday but not yet translucent and glowing. The trees and grasses were still solid in their bright colors. Four or five species of pink, red, yellow and white small flowers were blooming everywhere. Lying on my stomach, seeing the world through flower stems, it was a different reality from looking down from above while hiking past. The flower stems rose above eye level with purple violets scattered beneath them. There were two levels of vertical form: the dense slender shrub and flower stems were at one scale and the relatively gigantic turkey oak and pine tree trunks passing through the flowers up to the sky were the other. Black vase-shaped seed heads had tiny red and pink spots. Trimmed with white hairs and backlit by the sun, they glowed like rubies. A layer of bracken fern fronds floated above the low ground cover of runner oak and wire grass. Strands of spider silk shimmered in a faint breeze as the sun caught them and then disappeared as they blew the other way. Even a few feet in elevation totally changes the way the world is constituted or the way we think it is.

Since I could see only a few feet in front of me, I concentrated on a big slash pine at eye level where the trunk emerged from the ground and swelled into a buttress. It was obvious that this living entity had exploded up out of the ground and into air and sunshine. These trees were all dynamic energy-filled systems despite their immobility. That apparent motionlessness was only a function of our differing time frames.

Six species of butterflies brightened the landscape at different seasons. This beauty is not just there for human admiration or to inspire sermons on God's perfection, even though biology developed out of natural history and natural history evolved out of natural theology, which consisted of nature inspired sermons on God's perfection. Rather, their flashing splendor is for the usual mundane needs of life — to provide protection, attract mates of the right species, blend in with the plant they sit on. Many of the most brilliant are poisonous and their color warns would-be predators not to bother. The dancing hovering flight pattern makes it hard for a predator to catch a butterfly. With an average adult lifespan of only two weeks — the migrating generation of monarchs lives longer than other generations— they spend it feeding, mating and reproducing. And yet in butterflies, those biological needs are met with the most splendid extravagance. As a class, insects have explored every possible evolutionary extreme. But butterflies are the magic specialists — in them the magic that underlies the world and mostly flows unseen is made manifest.

A butterfly house is a glass building, a shining gem of sun and sky, forest and waterfall and flowers. Within this crystal palace, the essence of summer is captured as the butterflies dance in their miniature tropical rain forest. They have surely attained butterfly heaven, surrounded by flowers, fruit, sugar- water, sunshine and mist. The same world that can build such a wondrous place now sees butterflies fading away, as we replace rain forest with cow pasture, turn trees into waste paper, destroy the intricate fabric of wild communities. As they disappear, what are we losing? They are critical as pollinators of plants and as food for other species, and their loss — like the loss of any species — adds to the great unraveling of this living planet. And yet butterflies are more. They are the wonder, the beauty, the power and the magic of the universe dancing before our eyes. If we cannot see that magic then surely we deserve the bleak world we will have when they are gone.

A deep awareness of the living grass and gnarly old-growth pines arose and occasionally turned into a focused intense seeing that stopped time and was not voluntary or casual. Transpersonal awareness is closer at hand in forests, oceans, deserts and mountains. The energy of a desert, of wind, of sky and mountains is a powerful blatant sweeping force with life dancing like a spirit on its shoulders. The energy of the lush wet country, however, is a more subtle delicate thing, the energy of iridescent comb jellies, of flowers and butterflies, of the mind of a wasp making its nest against a tree branch.

Several days later, I returned, mostly to see if such an experience could be recaptured at all. The answer was yes and no. The flowers and butterflies still danced— it was still beautiful. But it wasn't misty and the light was subtly changed. I was not exactly the same person, the energy was different somehow. It was its own moment, not a replay of an earlier one. No two moments are the same and magic is tricky stuff. It's not out there so much as it's within us. It's more a level of awareness than anything else. What we experience as magic is just being totally open to the situation. When the opening doesn't occur, we can still admire the beauty and the ecological intricacy of the place.

Butterflies are the magic specialists but the magic places are freshwater springs and mountain waterfalls. The magic of the world comes and goes. It's not rare but it's usually unpredictable, hard to capture. Florida's freshwater springs are an exception to this rule — where the ground water remains clean, they are a kaleidoscope of crystal, emerald and sapphire color, swirling glittering gems in the forest. Throwing coins into fountains is a survival of the ancient pagan custom of throwing offerings to the gods that were believed to live in springs in ancient Europe.

One spring was deep in the refuge forest. Not easy to get to, it was an hour in and an hour hike out again. The path started next to a highway and ran through open sunny long-leaf pine for a while. Then it dove into shady hardwood forest. The canopy closed; the trees were huge and ringing with bird calls. The occasional blazes on the trees barely kept me from getting hopelessly turned around. That's all they were supposed to do; you're obviously expected to know what you're doing out here.

Finally I got there, hot and ready for a swim. Palm trees lined the shore, standing out from the deep green surrounding swamp. As I appeared at the edge, a little alligator slid off its sunning log and discreetly disappeared as did its much bigger mamma under the bushes on the far side. In Asian temples, carved dragons are everywhere. Unlike the fire breathing European dragons at war with dragon slayers, Asian dragons are benevolent wise spiritual beings who hold in their jaws the orb of enlightened mind and encourage us to spiritual growth. I hoped these alligators were of the Asian lineage as I dove into the spring.

There was no sign that any human had been there since the Indians, and I was grateful for the hike that only let in those willing to make the effort. Something this special never comes free. Swimming out from a rock ledge with a face mask, I was suspended 60 or 70 feet above the mouth of a cave, the source of the cold clear water. Spotted gar and a few sunfish moved slowly just below the surface. It was hard to decide whether to remain below the surface, merging with the spring's own reality of white limestone and crystal water or to watch the sunlight dancing and flashing on the water in the world of air and color above it. The spring was a crystal transparent gem of blue water, white sand and emerald green mats of underwater grasses. The words of a Navaho prayer came to mind: With beauty before me I walk/ with beauty behind me I walk/with beauty below me I walk/ with beauty all around me I walk/ It is finished in beauty.

Inside another spring on another day, I perched like a giant wetsuited bird on a submerged tree limb in a crashing thunderstorm, looking up at the surface tension where each rain drop stretched the mirrored ceiling of the spring into a field of continuously forming and vanishing upside-down silver domes. A vertical lime rock ridge rose between the two bottomless holes through which water poured out of the ground and to the surface. The rock outcrops were cliffs of a sculptured convoluted complexity that was almost biological.

Swimming over to the shore, I sat down, warm in my wet suit. On the air side of reality, the rain came in a rush of silver streaks. It was a riot of flashing, dancing explosions as the drops hit the spring water, moving out into the river it created anew each moment. Then lightning exploded a little too close, signaling the end of the sitting period.

The seasons of the land were the familiar ones of summer and winter, but those of the spring had to do with flood and low water, inundation in cold blackness or glittering blue transparency. Six months later, the world had turned until summer thunderstorms were swept away by an incisive north wind. Blazing cold sunlight turned the scattered clouds to silver and gilded the bare gray and white branches of the surrounding forest as well. Downstream from the spring, thousands of tiny blazing golden fires danced on the surface as the water flowed over the tips of submerged miniature jungle in the spring run, micro rapids to challenge the water striders' skill.

The creek that drained the gum and cypress flood-plain forest behind the spring was flowing following several days of cold winter rain. The vibrant living spring itself was as jeweled and clear as always but cold black swamp water poured into the run along one bank, forming an eddying flowing frontier with the clear warm water. Down in the jungle of leafy waterweed, the colder denser swamp water lay puddled like patches of reddish brown fog in the blue-green world of the spring run. A gar lurked in the fog. From its darkness, the big predator could strike without warning. Bass and turtles ambled about, looking vaguely at loose ends. A pair of grass carp — 3 feet long, fat gray goldfish with blades of grass dangling from their mouths like cigarettes— stared stolidly at me with placid herbivore energy that could never conceive of needing something to do. There was grass, they ate it, what else could there be?

Beneath a mosaic of blue water and black tree reflections, green and gold eel grass waved sinuously in the current of clear sparkling water. Grey cypress trunks and the vertical lines of reeds and tree trunks framed the river banks. The river bed was full of rare native underwater plants and tiny black snails that grazed algae off the sand grains and limestone outcrops on the river bed. Herons and egrets, woodpeckers and anhingas perched on the trees and a pair of eagles soared overhead. Huge old bald cypress stood like sentinels in the river in front of smaller black gum trees.

Later I paddled a canoe down the spring run. The day had become nearly overcast, and away from the spring itself the dark swamp water had flooded the normally clear shallow run. Black water, gray forest and sky made a bleak winter like landscape in which even the image of a spring disappeared. But then the sun reappeared and in the suddenly blue sky, the last red/green clumps of needles on the cypress trees hung like Christmas ornaments. Unlike the intense blue of the spring that reflected only itself, the black water surface became a multicolored high contrast mirror, streaked with green, red and blue reflections of forest and sky.

A spring-run river is a gentle intimate place, the woods full of small song birds. Maple leaves were vivid scarlet against the blue sky and white clouds. Turtles were ten deep on every log, little ones perched on top of big ones. The pickerel weed and sagittaria marshes along the lakeshore were a huge bloom of purple and white flowers.

Manatees slowly drifted upstream, grazing their underwater meadows as schools of mullet, needlefish, and sheepshead darted under the canoe. It was hard to see through the glitter of the late afternoon sun but there was definitely something big and gray near the river bank. I turned the canoe and eased closer to a manatee and her calf. Mamma was grazing on the eelgrass, occasionally raising her head to breathe while the calf seemed to be asleep. Adults average 10 feet in length and weigh about 1,000 pounds. Only four species of sea cows survive today. This one was the West Indian manatee. They looked like small gray submarines cruising slowly through the clear water, gently flexing their broad paddle shaped tails. They winter in warm springs and then travel up and down the coastal sea grass beds in the summer.

Nature is so much bigger than the individual ego and is so ancient that my individual fears become irrelevant and disappeared. What was the role of a human mind in this moment and place? Perhaps it was to simply perceive that even though humans are the mental specialists on the planet, human mind is not separate and apart from all the rest of earth's conscious mind. There was only joy and gratitude to be part of a system that creates such natural beauty even though the death of individuals is part of it.

In our focus on pollution and saving the environment, we sometimes forget to give ourselves credit. As a society, we really do try — some of us, a little bit — to do the correct thing. Not all of us, perhaps, but enough so that the springs and flowers and butterflies were still there on fresh sweet mornings as they had been for who knows how many millions of years. And if that's so, then maybe some of the damage we've done elsewhere on the planet really is accidental. Perhaps we did it in ignorance more so than from indifference. And as we come to understand the planet better, maybe we'll repair some of that damage someday. At least, we're beginning to think about the possibility. Maybe the frontier values of subdue and plow really are being replaced with a more subtle, wiser approach to the rest of the planet.

CHAPTER 6

KYOL CHE

Hindrances are formidable and habits are deeply ingrained. Contemplation is weak and the mind drifts.

Zen Master Chinul

The contemplative traditions of both eastern and western religions move the individual from awakening experiences and illuminative insights to personality transformation to a life in which one's activities are an expression of spiritual awareness. Finding a way to help others is different for each of us. Why did Jesus serve the poor? Perhaps it had something to do with that forty day solitary retreat in the desert. The only thing we really can know about Jesus' life or Buddha's life is that something happened mentally and as a result of it these great spiritual leaders devoted the rest of their lives to teaching their insights. The emphasis is not on what happened but on what you do as a result of what happened. And we don't really have to rely on the fragmentary accounts of Buddha's life or Jesus' life. The opportunity to experience it directly is always before us. All we have to do make the time and make the effort.

In the Zen tradition in which I practiced meditation, the heart of the training is a ninety-day monastic retreat called Kyol Che or Tight Dharma. Unlike solo retreats, the power of a group retreat and conforming to an external schedule that isn't always comfortable means that negative opinions and mental resistance to what is happening will quickly appear. That in turn will show us exactly how our endless opinions, our likes and dislikes, only serve to make living in each moment with what is harder than it really needed to be. We can literally see the unhappy opinionated thinking mind that constantly judges everything creating extra suffering as we watch it on the meditation cushion. It is very difficult to experience this in any other setting, and seeing that is one of the most important lessons of a rigorous formal temple based Zen practice.

I had wanted to attempt a kyol che for years but family obligations had made it impossible. In my 60th year and with the boys grown up, it was clear that if it was ever going to happen, I had better get busy while I was still able. The cost was amazingly modest, and so I left the Gulf Coast forests, marshes and sea grasses and headed north to the Providence Zen Center in Rhode Island where Winter Kyol Che would begin a few days after the New Year. Housed in a huge century old rambling building, the center was staffed by a few resident laypeople and monks. Periodically the place was deluged with waves of visitors from around the country, Europe and Israel who washed in for retreats or ceremonies and then washed out again after the event.

A full moon, the first of four that would come and go during the retreat, floated in the eastern sky as we retreat participants left the main Zen center building, walked past a pond and up a hill to the traditional Korean-style monastery building where we would sit and explore the nature of mind for the next three months. A flock of Canada geese drifted serenely over the pond which was still unfrozen despite it being January in Rhode Island.

A few minutes later, however, I sat in a tiny bare cell with only a futon on the floor, a sleeping bag and one-half of a small closet. When my roommate arrived and took the other futon, one foot away from mine, I would have approximately twenty-five square feet of personal space in which to live for the next three months. The entire time would be spent in silence except for periodic interviews with the Zen Master. Monasteries have existed for thousands of years but now that I had moved into one, I was deeply uneasy. What on earth had I gotten myself into? As with most rural Buddhist temples, the forest was right outside but the climate was too cold to live there without walls, roofs and furnaces. The Zen center seemed like the outer zone, the monastery was the inner zone and the interview room at the monastery where I would face the challenges of the Zen Master seemed like the inner core of the whole physical place.

A monastery is a place apart from the world of daily life, and a retreat is an attempt to get away from the myriad details of daily life for a little while, but those details come with us inside our heads anyway. Hoping to experience mental stillness, we find instead that thinking becomes a torrent. It's not unusual to sit and obsess about personal issues all through the retreat. Meditation becomes an interplay of thinking mixed with occasional moments of stillness and sudden beauty. The job to be done here was inside the head, to see how the mind makes happiness and struggle and to learn to better manage it. Zen is about how you keep your mind moment to moment or more precisely to realize how mind functions moment to moment without inserting "you keep."

Verbal thought is so dominant that it normally blocks other alternate mental states from arising, but in a long meditation retreat, we learn to disassociate conscious awareness from conceptual thought and emotions. Mental awareness may slowly become more clear and calm until eventually it may for a moment give up chattering to itself and become still. Prolonged silence can reduce the verbal ego-based personality until one perceives its transitory impermanent fleeting nature. If the analytical rational side of the mind becomes mentally still for a long enough period of time, then without the continuous stream of thinking that creates it, the individual self-identity sometimes drops away, time and space and sensory input are gone. Whenever it fades away, moment-to-moment awareness of what is actually happening and knowing what to do in that moment is more likely to appear.

In daily life we act out our unspoken griefs and ego needs and angers all the time in an unaware fashion. We are also usually unaware that that is the very thing that keeps us unhappy. Thinking becomes the servant of desire, comfort and ego. Intuitive insight is valid only when done in a rigorous manner that has already stripped away ego-based delusions. Daily life is always presenting us with new challenges so we must keep doing this practice throughout life if we want to stay mentally clear. Eventually, as painful mental states weaken, more energy and happiness appears.

After doing this work and resolving old unresolved sources of suffering that we have carried with us for years, it then becomes more possible to begin to approach the core of the inside job: seeing what is beyond personal identity. It is possible to become still to the point that the ego-based self disappears for a moment and what is left is the experience of what we are that underlies ego.

The sheer length of time was what was unique about kyol che. To make a fundamental change in a lifetime's mental habits is not a trivial challenge. It would be impossible to do this work at this level of intensity in any other setting. Shorter retreats give useful insight but not sufficient time to reprogram the brain. To get the results of this slow personality transformation treatment, you simply have to stay for a long time. Leave too soon and you are not changed.

The kyol che began at 4:30 the next morning with one hundred and eight prostrations, full bows from a standing position to hands and knees and then back up, sutra chanting and meditation for three hours before breakfast. All the priestly ritual of lighting candles and incense at the altar was similar to what priests have done for millennia. In most other systems, however, its purpose is often to placate or ask favors from some deity. Here it was part of an effort to better comprehend reality without first creating some theological truth to be accepted on faith. Zen may be unique in world religions that way.

I sat on a cushion in front of huge windows that overlooked the pond and the Zen center building on the other side of the pond. At daybreak the geese came honking and soaring through falling rain, banked around the pond, stalled and fell like stones onto the water with wings held out to break their fall An otter swam along the shore as playing squirrels chased each other back and forth on the steep blue-tiled monastery roof. Thundering back and forth, they sounded like a herd of elephants overhead. I might be indoors but outside the rhythms of nature never stopped.

At breakfast, Zen Master Dae Kwang had a few words to share.

"How can we prioritize the present moment? We are never separate; we are all part of everything else so in helping others you are helping yourself. Letting go of the sense of "I my me" just perceive clearly and function correctly. Life is lived between the stimulus and the response. Don't make, don't hold, don't check, don't attach to anything, just be awake. We usually value our thinking more than we value the actual experiencing of life but practice means converting knowledge to wis-dom. Our inside job is to learn how to do that and our outside job is to be of service in some way, but they are exactly the same job. With the human body comes the illusion that we are separate from all else and we need to manipulate or fix it but that is not the case. Moment by moment just give yourself to the situation – holding back mentally reaffirms the illusion of separation. Do what you are doing 100% until you are that activity. Then you yourself become the unfolding universe. As for everyday checking, judging and thinking, just don't feed it and it will dissolve. A long retreat is where you learn how to really do this, thereby converting knowledge to wisdom. It's the best gift you can ever give yourself."

Meals were eaten in silence in the same spot in which we sat to meditate. The bland monotonous diet of grains, soup, salad, tea, raisins and nuts was the way humans had eaten for 8,000 years and was probably the first time I had ever been so free of sugar and caffeine. Afterward we were assigned jobs for the one-hour work period that we would do each day. I was sent back down to the main Zen center to do whatever housework needed doing there each day: vacuuming one day, cleaning windows the next, cleaning the altar of the main meditation hall the next. It was a little like commuting to a job.

Hiking down the hill to the Zen center for work practice, I was irritable from lack of sleep. Why had I paid good money to mop the floors, sleep on the floor, eat identical plain meals every day, and have every moment of the day regulated? Why couldn't we rest a little as needed? If you cure the disease of personal suffering and frustration and grief, it doesn't seem necessary to keep coming back to the hospital ICU of a long retreat, but what seems cured on the surface often has deep roots and it will flare up again when least expected. And a retreat is a multipurpose experience – it'll not only cure the disease, it will also reveal the other side of practice, the ability to see reality more and more clearly and to occasionally shape shift into mental states of great wellbeing.

In beginning to practice, people encounter Zen's unusual paradoxical teaching style and language. People may read lots of Zen books and develop some conceptual understanding. Attaining, however, means experiencing the reality of how our mind really works, internalizing it and recognizing it within our self. Whatever intellectual ideas we brought to the retreat about practice or Zen evaporate as we learn to let go of conceptual thought, become still and see what arises out of that stillness. Instead of increasing some theoretical understanding we have to let it go, replacing ideas with experience – mostly the messy hard specifics of how we create and can manage our own suffering. In doing so, we see experientially the accuracy of this particular spiritual path. Attaining means do you know your job, are you doing your job? Actualizing means living out of concrete experience until it is second nature and requires no further thinking or analysis. Attaining and actualizing are the business of a long retreat. At any point along the way, sudden non-verbal flashes of experience and insight – the magic moments – punctuate the process and keep you coming back.

The shallow puddles from the earlier rain were just starting to freeze and were full of delicate new ice needles, some lanceolate and some in star bursts. At the edges of the big puddles, new ice formed scalloped white patterns where air bubbles were trapped under it. Micro-striations in the clear ice made tiny golden lines of sunlight on the brown leaves under the water. Mental stillness is like new ice on a pond, thin at first and easily broken. It takes a while before the delicate brittle ice crystals become strong, but one thing we had here was time.

The forest was an uproar of birds singing. Who'd have thought that songbirds sing in the middle of winter in New England? As I walked past the main building, a honking racket erupted behind me as the geese came barreling across the pond in a straight line and then lifted off like a squadron of heavy planes in formation. They wheeled above my head in the sunny cold blue sky and then disappeared beyond the trees. By the time I got to the front door of the Zen center, I had forgotten about being crabby.

After work period, most of the rest of each day was spent sitting motionless in meditation in a large open room with cushions in a rectangle around the huge altar. A retreat day had many different things in the schedule but they all kept rotating back to sitting. Since the daily schedule never changed, the long retreat was an eternal now with no past or future. Time had quit flowing forward and was spinning in a circular eddy that would make 90 revolutions before it resumed its journey onward. The absolute sameness of each day's routine was a blank backdrop against which each person's mental movie played out with minimal distractions. Do it long enough, I hoped, and the mind might finally run out of new mental material, settle down, become quiet and then notice NOW. It hadn't happened yet but surely in 90 days it would. Intense vivid late afternoon sunlight poured into the dharma room, filling the room with shiny brass and bright colors. That turned into a pale clear evening sky with tree silhouettes a stark black against the yellow afterglow of the sunset. Sensory perception was becoming more intense every day.

After a week of sitting motionless for hours a day, however, I had an endless backache and pain in the side. I'd never been so exhausted for so long in my life. The fatigue was like a fog. It cleared out and everything was ok for a few minutes and then it came rolling back until I was ready to give up again. No altered mental states, no past life memories, just exhausted, exhausted, exhausted. I switched from the traditional cushion on the floor to a chair. The goal was to get through the retreat, never mind style and appearances.

This was clearly my last chance to try this. After 20 years of coming here, this practice style was getting physically beyond me. This body was like an old car with high miles that had also been through a wreck with some serious health problems. I was getting too old and stiff to do this daily schedule that went from 4:30 AM to 9:40 PM daily in a training system developed centuries before anybody ever heard of weekends.

In meditation, you make a problem, you get a problem, and that was exactly what I was doing by worrying about whether to stay or go and what I would or would not get from this effort to take back home to daily life. The first challenge was obviously going to be the body, but the second challenge would be the endless mental resistance that also kept arising. Even though I had done lots of shorter retreats with the same daily schedule, now I was less tolerant of being pushed so hard, no longer willing to be challenged in the interview room, told what to do every minute, grit through fatigue and pain. There was a strong perception that time was now too short for putting up with things that didn't quite fit. But neither did I want to quit so soon after waiting years to do this.

The restrictive retreat environment created an intense mind of dissatisfaction where we could really see how the process works. Stay here three months and everything that could come up would come up and could then be faced and dealt with. The mind of dissatisfaction is much more subtle and hard to see when sabotaging well-being in daily life. If I left early, there would still be hidden issues that hadn't yet surfaced. This practice was literally about cleaning the mind.

The normal times to enter or leave the retreat were on Saturday mornings. If things weren't going better this time next week, maybe I would leave on that Saturday. Ok, I thought, here's the plan: first get the body functional – get knees and lower back ok in a chair, then wean myself from the chair back to the cushion and still be OK physically; then get the mind quiet and stop chattering to myself; then watch the quiet mind and see what happens.

"How will I make it to evening chanting?" I thought despairingly. Lying on my futon in the dark during a short break after supper, I psyched myself up to stay and do it. I didn't have the strength anymore to face this practice without help. HELP!!!!! I began to pray to any and all powers for strength and energy to continue. I prayed to all the unknown forces that we label Bodhisattva, Jesus Christ and all the other names human beings have invented through the centuries.

"Any and all powers that can help – please help me get through this peacefully. I make it a prison with my mind. Let me make it a wonderful experience with my mind, oh, please!!!"

"Don't make anything with your mind!" came back a voice from who knows where.

I went outside and marched up and down the hill three times under a crescent moon. A great horned owl was calling and the first stars were out. The evening star was low in west.

"If I give up and leave, I'll be an old woman from now on. Keep going! Don't quit! This retreat is a gateway to the Big Thing - do you want to experience it or not? Have you just been lying to yourself all these years? I AM STRONG I WILL DO THIS! EVERYTHING NO PROBLEM! Ride this great dark dharma horse, dammit!" When the huge temple bell rang during evening chanting, I could feel the sound waves on my ear drums.

By the end of the week, the pond was frozen solid as the nighttime lows hit 8 degrees F or so. Liquid water was like a shiny mirror, and the semi-opaque ice was like cracked glass. The thinking mind continued to drive me nuts, totally out of control like a wild horse that I couldn't stop. Mostly it was the mind that wanted to leave the retreat but I didn't particularly want to go home either. Maybe I could get to the airport, rent a car and go up to Acadia National Park in Maine. But what if there was a blizzard! I didn't know anything about driving in snow and ice and it was January in New England, for Chrissake! And roaring around the highways was fun but didn't create deep-seated well-being, just some entertainment mixed with a hollow sense of rattling around. And it was too expensive to make a habit of anyway. If the mind could not be controlled here and now it never would be and I would never be happy wherever I ran away to or however many trips I took.

How many mental squalls would come and go during this retreat? They were just repetitive speeches about what I didn't like. The mind of dissatisfaction has many different clothes. Coming here was an effort to diagnose and treat the illness of mind going negative and thereby sabotaging actualized, buoyant compassionate moment-to-moment mental states.

That afternoon, the horse got the bit in its teeth and ran away with me. I had to fall back to just enduring the mental squall but not acting on it. It was like being in the middle of the Pacific Ocean in a canoe. Squalls came mostly during sitting sessions, not at any other time. Exhaustion, pain and physical struggle always triggered it, but what other underlying emotional issues were also there? As soon as I let the mind wander the least bit from watching the breath or saying a mantra, the thinking mind was right back to wanting to bail out, with diatribes about everything I thought was wrong with the situation, exactly what it did at home whenever I focused on what seemed to be a problem there.

The buoyant compassionate personality that is the mark of a mature Zen practice comes from being free of self-created mental suffering. A woman three cushions away to the left was my height and weight and hair color and cut. She looked grim, sad and determined just as I so often had and probably did in that moment. Seeing her, I saw myself. Keep trying! At home, when physical discomfort arises we tend to it immediately so we don't see how it creates the mind of dissatisfaction. If I could learn to control that here, then maybe I'd be able to better manage it at home where the process was much more subtle and hard to see clearly. If you don't give life everything you've got, you'll never know how much you have to give.

By the next week, I had calendar mind, counting up the weeks, days and hours until the retreat would be finished and doing it over and over. The unchanging daily schedule would create a sense of timeless cycling if I could let go of calendar mind but instead I made waypoints to maintain a sense of time passing forward. It was a prolonged low level mental squall that would be a part of life until the end of the retreat. At an interview, I complained to Zen Master Dae Kwang Sunim about all the unstoppable negative thinking that hit every time I sat down.

"Take away those thoughts and what is there?" the Zen Master asked

"Compassionate awareness?" I guessed, feeling like a kid in school.

"Take away compassionate awareness and what is left?" he demanded. I held my sore back and made a face.

"Correct! It is so simple but people make it complicated. It's just being totally present with what in fact is without adding editorializing."

"Sit with a bright mind," he added, "eyes open, alert to everything that occurs, and say the mantra 100%, not by rote. Say it with a buoyant mind. Moment-to-moment mind spontaneously arises out of mental stillness. Don't have any agenda like what you hope to take home from this in three months."

The brain is very good at identifying, analyzing, and solving problems. That is its job, but when we treat our lives as an endless string of problems to be solved and obstacles, when we focus predominately on what is wrong with life, then we destroy any possibility of wellbeing, especially if it is a situation that cannot be easily changed and is something we just have to work with as it is. Fix what can be fixed but come to terms with the reality of what cannot be changed.

That afternoon a Korean nun gave a talk, describing the training nuns got in traditional Asian temples. Only after six years of monastic training could they attempt to sit a kyol che. For four of those years, the only words they could speak were "yes" and "sorry." What on earth was I complaining about here? A monk described a long solo retreat he had just finished a few weeks before this kyol che had begun. He was doing a thousand prostrations a day and semi-fasting. One day, he had opened the wood stove in his cabin to add some logs. He poked the fire, sat back in a state of total exhaustion, and suddenly his mind had opened into Enlightenment. Tears of joy came into his eyes as he tried to relate the story to us.

Seeing the real monastic vocations of the monks and nuns in the retreat as they told their stories at the weekly Saturday talks, I realized that their commitments to this way of life were far beyond what I had. Maybe it was necessary to come here, struggle, see them and also see the grim/sad/determined faces of people like me who were lost in their personal problems. Even without speech, we all developed the tight emotional bonds of shared adversity.

It had snowed that morning, just enough to turn the world white. After the talk, the snow was melting quickly in the bright sunlight but was still on the grey rocks by the door, part of an island of grey rock, green moss and white snow. Big drops of water fell from the roof as the snow melted. Each drop hit a wooden step and a circular spray of tiny silver water droplets exploded outward like a flower or a fireworks explosion. The squirrels were storming about, chasing each other across the roof again. One crept carefully along the edge of the roof, hanging upside down. It passed in front of the low afternoon winter sun, unaware of the golden white blaze of sunlight pouring through its tail fur. Life at home, like life here, was a mixture of riches and hardness. This tough mental and physical training gave the ability to cope with the hardness and appreciate the riches.

When I rather proudly announced this insight to the Zen Master at the next interview, he immediately shot it down. "A three-day retreat, a ninety-day retreat, they are all the same – a split second! If you expect your mind to be somehow different on the last day of this retreat than it is today, you're wrong! Sitting is absolutely simple but nobody wants that, so we make up stuff about it. You have to not make up anything!"

I brought up the monk's story about doing 1000 bows a day and said, "I have a camp in the woods for solo retreats but I can't physically do 1000 bows a day, so how should I practice there?"

"Just keep moment-to-moment mind and a thousand bows a day is not necessary," he answered. "When the mind is still, sitting still is not a problem. When mind is chattering it is very difficult."

February 1st and the dawn light revealed new snow. Individual flakes on the rocks by the door looked like white lichens. Falling snow covered the forest and pond and meadow. It was all white against a dark purple sky. Thirty minutes later as it got lighter, the landscape paled to the usual white/grey/brown of winter. Pretty soon, snow was pouring down so hard that the air was a white fog, and by afternoon there was only watch-the-snowflakes meditation. If I were not here all the beauty of the snowy days would not have been experienced. The snow turned to rain and that night everything froze into a solid glaze of ice. A rock-solid white snow/ice pavement formed with a bumpy texture from when it had been

ZEN IN A WILD COUNTRY

slush. It was not slippery at all. The next morning, frozen water droplets hung from every branch, each with a tiny sun blazing at its heart. The sun revealed the intense red of geraniums and a flash of blue fire from a glass hanging in a green spider plant on the sun porch of the Zen center dharma room. Walking back to the monastery after work practice, a gust of wind blew a shower of snowflakes off a bush and into my face.

"Here it all is but I don't get it," I thought glumly, staring into the oncoming horizontal river of snowflakes. Drop "I don't get it," just keep "Here it all is," came the internal voice.

The schedule was a simple thing. I made it tough with my mind, I made it easy with my mind. Vacuuming at the next work practice I was back to thinking about rental cars, was not actualized and buoyant while doing the vacuuming. The mind of dissatisfaction was still running the show and the job of this retreat wasn't done at all. The main thing keeping me here was that I didn't want to go home until I had changed enough to be able to be at peace there, not just outdoors but also in the daily struggles of life. I hope today is a better day than yesterday, I thought, but that doesn't just float down out of the sky like a snowflake, it depends on how we keep our minds. Do a better job on that and it will be a better day.

What difference would staying here eight more weeks make? The only way to see would be to stay. Three months didn't seem like an unreasonable time for a task as ambitious as trying to reinvent my mind. A calligraphy on the wall said "Three days of looking at self/thousand year treasure; one hundred years seeking power and status/ things turn to dust in a moment."

People have struggled to master this mental art for thousands of years. An ancient Buddhist text, the Dhammapada makes it clear how difficult it is:

"Even as a fletcher straightens an arrow, so the wise one straightens the mind which is fickle and unsteady, difficult to guard and difficult to control. Just as a fish pulled out of water and cast on land thrashes and thrashes, even so the mind while leaving the realm of delusion. Wonderful indeed it is to subdue the mind difficult to subdue, swift moving and seizing whatever it desires. Difficult to detect and extremely subtle is this mind, seizing whatever it desires; let the wise one guard it. A guarded mind brings happiness." I had thought my mind was reasonably subdued but this retreat was showing otherwise.

To break out of the mental thorns, I tried to generate visual images of my favorite outdoor places in Florida. A picture arose of the blue and white sea floor of a deep reef off of the Marquesas Keys, west of Key West, a place I had visited years before with a team of shark researchers. A huge silver barracuda hung motionless in front of me. At night we had turned off the dive lights and swum by moonlight on the sea floor. Blue sparkles of bioluminescent plankton had swirled around our flippers as we swam. When the slap of a stick signaled the end of the meditation period I slowly and reluctantly returned to the room.

When we treat life as a problem to be solved and hyper-focus on what is wrong, we destroy mental well-being. We obsess about a topic, endlessly repeat some analysis and jump to imaginary worst case possibilities that usually don't materialize after all. We fantasize imaginary disasters, figure out solutions to problems that aren't our job to solve, endlessly remind ourselves of what we don't like and what we have failed to achieve. We ignore the positives of life, rush through the present situation to get to the next situation, stay stuck in old perceptions even when they are out of date because the situation has changed.

If I followed the mind of dissatisfaction out of this retreat, I'd never master it at home. It came and went in concert with the pain in my side and back. As soon as the pain started, I wanted to leave and thinking served that desire by reinforcing it. When pain went, it all subsided. Pay more attention to all the things that gave me energy every day: stretching out to rest the back, walking up and down the hill to work every morning, the food, sunlight in the dharma room and the stained glass reflections, the colors of the altar, the sound of birds singing in a New England winter even when it was snowing, the rainbow diamonds of snow crystals sparkling in the sun, the hush and stillness of snow falling in the woods, the glowing vibrant green of moss growing under clear ice and white snow, squirrels romping over the monastery roof like a herd of buffalo.

Outside at five AM after bows, a rooster crowed in the cold air and darkness. It did that every day with no doubt, no hesitation or wondering what else it should be doing. Grateful for the rooster's wonderful teaching, I went back inside for morning practice. While it was still dark, the altar and the gold Buddha were reflected in the dark mirror of the window glass and the moon was shining through the reflection.

As it got lighter, the reflections faded until only the full round moon remained, sailing across the clear dawn sky with altar and Buddha disappeared.

After breakfast, walking to the Zen center, the pain in my side was gone but mind was still stuck counting the days. Perceiving this situation as grueling had quickly become a mental habit. I needed to be aware of the moments when that was not the case and stop automatically creating an exhausted mind out of habit. How is it just now? Can I do what I need to do in this moment? If the answer is yes, then just do it. Then no mental problem. Snow falls, white air. Snow stops, clear air. Each is complete, there's no need to prefer one over the other.

"I am trying to break a mental habit," I announced at the next interview.

"Don't do that!" the Zen Master said.

"It's the mind of dissatisfaction," I persisted.

"Don't be dissatisfied with the mind of dissatisfaction," he shot back, "don't try to make yourself anything, don't make any idea. If you think Anne is this – so what? If you think Anne is that – so what? Don't make anything. If you try to make something like "change a mental habit" then you aren't really free. Only keep what is this? Don't know and when you do something, do it one hundred per cent. Give me your dissatisfaction mind and I will take it out and throw it away," he added. And of course it did not exist in that moment and I could not produce it.

"Why does Buddhism have such a strong strain of negative life-denying overemphasis on suffering?" I demanded. "The marks of existence are non-self, suffering and impermanence but they are also joy, beauty, love, play and laugher. Impermanence also means new wonders are always appearing. Impermanence is the glory of the natural world. Impermanence is creativity!" I was on a roll and not about to quit.

"To call it nothing but suffering is a mistake," I continued. "Things disappear, other things appear. We love this world because it is our correct place while in the body. The joy that can come from experiencing beauty is feeling the rightness of being alive here and now. For everything that passes away, something else appears. Even old age, sickness and loneliness will disappear when death comes," I concluded triumphantly.

"But," said the Zen Master, "we latch to and cling to the positive and don't want to let go when the time comes to do that and then we suffer. Old age, sickness and death are neither negative nor positive; they just are what they are. That is the point of the Heart Sutra. We just don't like them so we make them negative. Some Buddhist teaching can be life-denying but Zen doesn't do that. It celebrates the beauty of nature constantly in Zen poetry. Too much metaphysics from you today!"

"What's wrong with metaphysics?" I demanded.

"Nothing," he answered, "but people get attached to their theory and then fight over it instead of keeping an open mind of inquiry and good will. That kills don't-know mind when keeping don't-know mind can lead to the experience of absolute reality."

"People come to Zen either to get something or to get away from something," he continued "but in fact you get nothing except what is already and always present and unnoticed. You get clarity and insight into your situation, up to and sometimes including perceiving true self."

"I think this is a young person's game," I groused.

"The mind is never young or old – start taking care of it. I've been doing kyol ches for 27 years."

"There must be something there then!"

"There is nothing there! That is why I keep doing them."

"Mind may not be young or old but the body sure as hell is!!" I snapped. He laughed and rang the bell, ending the interview.

The next day I used meditation methods from a traditional Buddhist text, *The Four Foundations of Mindfulness*, and mind became much quieter. Thoughts were mostly isolated and single, not a steady stream. I observed the sensations that led to the arising of a thought, especially the urge to stand up and observed the changing sensory experiences while walking around the room.

"This works! Now I know better what to do with the mind, so can I leave and do it at home?" the ego asked hopefully. But I had just realized this today. Suppose I had left yesterday and missed today? And what would arise tomorrow that I would miss if I left today?

The next morning, all the melt water from the day before was frozen solid at 16 degrees with new snow that fell on top of that. The trees had metallic silver sheaths when the rising sun hit the ice encasing their trunks. The snow was a solid frozen pavement with no crunching or squeaking, like cement everywhere. Rivers of ice ran where it was melting and running off yesterday.

By the middle of the retreat, the canoe had left mid-ocean and was over the outer continental shelf! Still a long way from land, at least it was in soundings. Was it across the ocean or just back to the same continent from which it set out? Coming to kyol che to see what lay beyond the mental surf zone of shorter retreats, I seemed to have forgotten that the waves of the open ocean were a lot bigger than they were near shore not to mention that the sharks were bigger and there be dragons and sea serpents as well! At least I could see how the powerful negative mental states of the last few days were impermanent, and would arise and pass away if I just waited them out without acting them out. One corner of the pond had thawed and the geese, which had bailed out when it froze solid, were back. They swam about breaking the ice to create open water and diving like dabbling ducks for plants.

Interviews with the Zen Master focused largely on trying to solve kong ans, the enigmatic riddles of the Zen tradition. From grand philosophical theories of Reality, kong ans bring our awareness back to the concrete specific details of this exact moment and this exact situation – they uncover the transcendent in each moment as it arises. There can sometimes be a little discussed non local psychic component to kong an practice in which something seems to leap between teacher and student as they face each other in the interview room. This is one reason why Zen is traditionally called mind to mind transmission without words and letters. Answering kong ans requires intuitive insight rather than rational analysis. It means finding what is completely alive in the moment of the story and in the moment of the encounter with the teacher. Exhausted and angry about being exhausted that morning, I was nowhere near any of that.

I sat down on a mat across from Dae Kwang Sunim who said

"A monk once asked Zen Master Pung Hol, 'Both speech and silence include separation and union. How can we be free and without fault?' Pung Hol said, 'I still remember Kong Nam in March. Many fragrant flowers where the partridges call.'"

"So how would you have answered that question?" he asked.

"I have no idea!" I said. "Why do we use these kong ans that just encourage the mind of I want?"

"So we can see it clearly. The human mind is like a bird. It is attracted or repelled by anything that comes before it."

What was the answer to the kong an? Don't know! Will I finish kyol che? Don't know! What will happen after it's over? Don't know! How long will I live in this body? Don't know! What else will happen before death? Don't know! What will happen at death? Don't know! What is this all about? Don't know! All of life is an unanswered kong an. The kong an just opens the don't-know door.

One kong an in particular was tough. Centuries ago in ancient China, the 5th Patriarch of Zen was looking for a successor to inherit his temple. He announced a poetry contest – whoever could produce a short poem that best expressed their grasp of the inexpressible would be the next teacher. The head monk offered a poem that said "Body is Bodhi tree/Mind is clear mirror's stand/Always clean, clean, clean/ Don't keep dust." An illiterate layman in the temple heard the poem and presented his own poem: "Bodhi has no tree/Clear mirror has no stand./Originally nothing./Where is dust?" The layman got the succession, but centuries later our founding teacher, Zen Master Seung Sahn, had said the winning poem wasn't quite on point either and wrote his own.

Now we had to find our founding teacher's answer to the challenge by recreating what he had written. I'd solved the first three lines a long time ago but had been stuck on the fourth line for years. Coming into the retreat I'd promised myself that at least I'd finish solving that poem kong an. But now, the retreat was well along, and every time I was sure I had it, my solution was wrong. Today's interview was more of the same. I was still stuck and extremely frustrated about it.

"The fourth line is becoming a sterile exercise," I complained after missing it yet again.

"It's sterile if you make it sterile with your thinking," said Dae Kwang Sunim. "Trees don't say they are beautiful or they are sterile. Any abstract concept like beauty or sterile is a mental creation. Underneath that is something wordless and absolute but you must stop thinking, verbalizing, generalizing to experience it."

A huge emotional mental squall arose that evening about having missed the kong an. The problem was convincing myself I had the right answer and wanting the right answer too much, I mused sourly. If it weren't for the kong an, I would be ok. "No!" said the voice. "If it weren't for 'I-want' mind, you'd be ok." No wonder some people believed in guardian angels. It felt like one was sitting on my shoulder. What was that voice? Was it just my own mind using a different form of talking to itself or was it something else? A lot of the kong ans posed a dualistic situation and then asked, "are these the same or different?" The solutions always lay in rejecting the apparent either/or in favor of a direct demonstration of concrete non analytical reality in that moment. So me and the voice, same or different? Who knows? Another unanswered kong an had appeared.

A public ceremony to mark the halfway point of the retreat and the beginning of Intensive Week was held a few days later. For the next 7 days we would add a midnight to 2AM sit to the already intense schedule. It was too icy for people in the community to drive up the hill to the monastery so we all hiked in a silent line to the Zen center in ice and snow in the dark. A hike in the dark! How wonderful to have a new thing happen. The lack of any novelty made sure that the only game in town was the one between our ears and didn't give the thinking mind anything extra to think about except what am I? A more diverse schedule would just be a distraction from the job of changing the mind around.

At the ceremony, we got a series of pep talks from people who had done a lot of long retreats. Intensive week is Buddha sitting under the tree vowing to attain or die. Do or die! I'd already made my decision about do or die. If it was time to die, I would rather do it at home with my family.

On his first 100-day solo retreat, the school's founding teacher, Zen Master Seung Sahn, had been told "You can die, go crazy or get Enlightenment." The first two options were obviously real, but the third seemed pretty remote. Die, go crazy or get Enlightenment doing this. Imagine going crazy, the mind totally out of control. That was scary. Well, hell, it is out of control, I snapped to myself. Just try to stay quiet on the cushion for more than one moment.

There are two levels of reality that we can perceive: the day-to-day material world and a transcendent underlying reality that is seen in brief glimpses. It's like pulling back the drapes in front of the window for just a second and getting a brief glimpse of what is beyond the window and then the drapes close again. Both levels are real and important. The day-to-day world is not a delusion or an illusion because it usually obscures the other reality. Rather, it is just a different plane of reality and one that is a constant flux of impermanent arising and dissolving phenomena whereas the other is unchanging. Perceiving what underlies it means we can function better in daily life.

Is all this hard work of religious practice, of trying to experience some transcendent state, just pushing the season? I wondered as the pep talks went on. Is it trying to force the mind into what it will naturally do anyway at death? Enlightenment and the Near-Death Experience can be very similar, so is the Enlightenment experience simply a premature induction of what happens at death? The most unnatural thing for the mind is not thinking and the most unnatural thing for the body is not moving. The only time those experiences happen together naturally is at death. Reduced sensory input, physical pain from the hours of sitting motionless and altered sleep patterns, all common as death approaches, are also induced in intensive Zen retreats. Maybe pain plus prolonged non-moving and non-thinking fools the brain into thinking the body is dead and triggers the neurological circuits that normally activate at death.

Those who experience these altered mental states describe very similar experiences and both experiences have similar effects on personalities afterward. In both the classic Zen Enlightenment experience and the Near Death Experience, it is virtually impossible to communicate the experience verbally to another person. It is as though the brain is a laptop but the overall program of Reality requires a supercomputer - the program is simply too big to run on the brain based laptop.

Descriptions of both states include sudden insight into questions of life's meaning, are impossible to accurately describe in words, involve feelings of no separation of self from the entire universe, the perception that unconditional love is at the root of all creation, a loss of any fear of death, deep peace, the perception that the experience is more real than anything in normal egocentric daily life, and often the ability to re-experience that state at will.

Researchers at the University of Montreal have been able to directly observe the brain activity of those who have had those experiences and have found that both the NDE and the Enlightenment experience produce the same changes in brain activity and neural circuits in areas associated with spiritual awareness and unconditional love. Both types of experience lead to the ability to consciously control brain wave activity and individuals do so in the same ways. Both subjectively and neurologically, the NDE and the spiritual Enlightenment experience are virtually identical. The NDE seems to blow open a door in the brain that normally opens only at death or after years of intense meditation practice. And Buddhism has traditionally held that the moment of death is a point when the Enlightenment experience is particularly accessible.

Yoga and meditation have been shown in repeated studies to lessen stress, lower blood pressure, reduce anxiety and improve mental alertness and wellbeing. There is now an increasing body of research that documents the ability of a meditation practice to change the physical brain. The human brain exhibits neuroplasticity, the ability to rewire itself in response to changes in its environment. This is accomplished by growing or pruning dendrites, the thousands of root like connective endings on a neuron that allow one neuron to communicate with others and create neural loops within the brain. After only a few months of daily meditation practice, areas of the brain associated with anxiety and fear, stress and anger, are less active while the areas associated with self-awareness, compassion, wellbeing and memory are strengthened. Age related memory loss and declines in social awareness also show improvement. These results are produced by the actual meditation techniques independently of any associated religious or philosophical beliefs. Buddhist monks and Catholic nuns with years of intensive meditation experience show very similar mental patterns relative to those who do not meditate.

Other neurological research has shown that the brain has two alternative neural circuits. One focuses on external events and tasks. When there is nothing going on externally, as in a meditation retreat, the second network, which focuses on personal thoughts and emotions becomes dominant. Normally one or the other is dominant but long term meditators often have the ability to keep both active simultaneously, resulting in a sense of merging or no separation of self and the external realities of the moment.

The brains of monastics who have practiced intensive meditation for years, regardless of religious affiliations or beliefs, differ from others in how the thalamus functions, in increases in the neurotransmitters dopamine and serotonin, and in different brain wave patterns such as increases in theta waves. There is elevated activity in the left prefrontal cortex which is involved in alertness and joyous emotions and a decline in activity in the areas of the right prefrontal cortex where anxiety, stress and sadness are centered.

Meditation is a form of farming and the crop is new dendrites in brain areas that are associated with wellbeing, empathy, peacefulness and other positive mental states. It is very subtle work sitting in a meditation hall, growing new dendrites. Feeling bored or restless means that we are not fully engaged in that work. Pain, fatigue and mental stress block it until we reach a tipping point and the pain, stress and grief abruptly become joy and well-being.

Whatever is happening at death is a natural cycle, as normal as infancy and adolescence, as flowers becoming seeds and dispersing. When he was near death, the school's founding teacher was asked why we must do hard practice. "We practice hard to see that hard practice is not necessary!" he had barked. If Enlightenment is simply a premature induction of the NDE, why not just wait until death when it may arise anyway? Why maintain churches, temples, organized religion, rituals, or a teaching tradition? Is all that merely an older, now obsolete expression of the phenomenon? Do we now have more precise language to use in considering this matter that can replace the traditional paradoxes, shouts, hits of a stick, kong ans and so on of ancient Zen practice? What's the rush?

Living daily life with the ego-based mind is natural and spontaneous, whereas letting go of thinking and cultivating wordless awareness is hard to do. Maybe the strong grip of ego-based mind is evidence that this stage of existence is not the time for transcendence. Maybe all the hard work of trying to experience some transcendent state is just pushing the season, trying to force the mind into what it will naturally do anyway at death. Why not just live this life in our normal ego-based state and leave the rest until its time has come? If there is an alternation of generations, the nonmaterial half and its unique forms of awareness will come in its own time.

But if we really want to know about these things, why wait around for death? Our days as we live them can be so much richer and happier with the extra clarity that comes from recognizing and letting go of neurotic mental habits. That happens with a spiritual practice regardless of whether transcendent awareness ever arises, so why continue to live in a confused and painful way?

Practice contributes to optimally living this life here and now in this body. Most of Zen practice is about perceiving and releasing the painful mental self- concepts that generally block transcendent awareness from arising. Intellectual metaphysical theories will not get this hard work done. Only through long term intense meditation practice can we clean up our personal messes enough to perceive what lies beyond the ego. If there is a purpose to being alive, an intensive meditation practice helps us to find it and then to proceed in a wiser way. Wait to deal with it all when the time comes and it may be too late as sickness takes its toll of energy. And in the moment when the mind shuts down in sickness and death, all the ideas, facts, and theories will become inaccessible. If we believe that our passing thoughts and feelings are who we are, that transition is likely to be very confusing. But if we have already perceived a little of the non-verbal forms of consciousness, then in that moment when brain based thought fades, we may be better able to experience the process. It is simply common sense to learn how to navigate the ship before we leave the familiar waters of our home port and proceed into the huge seas of the open ocean. And we need to do it while there is sufficient health, energy, strength and focus to get the job done. If the mind can stay focused in daily life, maybe it will remain more focused in the moment of death and allow a smoother transition into whatever might come next.

Finally, the idea that Enlightenment and the NDE are related may be accurate but it is only one of the many competing theories and ideas about what is reality or what meaning there might be to living a life time. If the actual experience should appear as a result of a spiritual practice, that is far more real, complete, satisfying and convincing than any theory.

The first day of Intensive Week, I actually felt more energy than on any day so far. The mind was much less frantic and there was no backache and no need to use a chair instead of a cushion. Gonna need that extra energy starting tonight at midnight, I thought. Before chanting there was not only energy but JOY JOY JOY! came in waves for no particular reason. Dharma energy! LET'S GET IT ON!

After the first midnight-to-two AM sitting, however, the 4:30 AM wakeup, bows, chanting and early sitting were almost impossible. Once again, the experience was different from any idea I might have had. Zen is all about experiencing, not ideas and theoretical images. I was soon back to a life of waiting for things to be over: how many minutes until we walk, how many sitting periods until a meal, how many days until the end of the week, how many weeks until the end of the retreat. A terrible mental squall struck during the afternoon sitting. It was the worst ever, beyond just thinking. I nearly ran out of there. Was it so intense due to sleep loss? It was hugely different from yesterday's joy. Would there now be emotional mood swings? What uproar over what was really nothing. So I sit here for a few more weeks. So what!? It didn't matter how many mental squalls came and went, just endure them. If I count over the remaining weeks 5000 times, so be it.

Just as mind makes the desire for recognition and meaningful work, it also makes the idea that life has a meaning and that we must get Enlightenment and discover what that meaning is. That was another idea too, an idea that Buddhism puts out there and I had soaked up years before. Quit pushing the season, I told myself. Let go of that idea too and just keep doing the practice. Quit checking how quickly or slowly results arise. Quit wanting something and then worrying about whether this effort will produce it!

"I'm starting to do loving-kindness practice," I said at the next interview. Creating a mental state of loving-kindness directed at various individuals was another traditional Buddhist meditation.

"Already a mistake!" he interrupted.

"Well," I persevered, "I learned that I have a lot of difficulty in simply feeling positive emotions."

"Old karma, old mental habits. Karma is just old mental habits and the future consequences of endlessly repeating them."

"Karma can be changed," I said. "Maybe we can't eliminate mental habits but we can replace painful ones with more positive helpful ones."

"The only way to change karma is to let go of it," he responded.

The problems and disappointments of life can teach valuable lessons, usually about things that we would never voluntarily try to learn. Since they are here, we might as well try to see what we can learn even as we keep trying to take actions to fix the problem. Eventually we can make new positive mental habits and create happiness for ourselves. It cannot come from suppressing and denying personal needs in a martyred way of life. Personal needs must also be recognized and met. A realized life is about how to live each day just as much as it is about experiencing occasional blissful mental openings. It is a mental habit.

"If we have to let go of all conceptual thought, what about the wisdom and insights that arise in meditation?" I demanded of the Zen Master.

"Let go of all conceptual thought – don't attach to ANY conceptual thought that arises. Thinking CAN'T get you there. It's like lifting yourself by the bootstraps - - it just won't work. If it is really wisdom, it'll be there."

"Not with my poor memory!"

"We think it is about memory but that is not where it is. That is the nature of our mind. It always tries to hold onto things or insights but as soon as you are trying to hold something in your mind you are no longer fully present in the moment and you lose the experience that is actually unfolding. This whole system is based on keeping the mind totally present in this moment and the next and the next for the rest of this lifetime and beyond that – so to do that you have to let things flow through."

Thinking may not get you to Enlightenment but the wisdom that arises makes navigating life a lot smoother and that is important too I thought rebelliously as I walked back to the meditation cushion.

After dinner, I went outside into the last red glow on the western horizon with a brilliant evening star just above it. The eastern sky was already dark. A half-moon was overhead and the stars were appearing one by one. The air had warmed to forty degrees and the fragrant smell of thawing wet earth was everywhere. The bells of a nearby Catholic Church and the warm glowing lights of the Zen center across the pond created a sense of enormous peaceful serenity. A bobbing point of light came around the pond as a nun with a flashlight walked from the Zen center to the monastery for evening chanting. Suddenly it was an enchanted place, abruptly breathtakingly imbued with sacred meaning, full of some sort of transcendent awareness. All the restlessness and urge to leave was gone in that moment of perfection. Why would anybody ever want to be anyplace else? It was a moment of total complete shimmering Enough Mind even though the sense of self and sensory input were still present. Mentally silent and full of gratitude, I answered the call to evening chanting.

Snow fell again that night. At dawn it was still snowing and all the horizontal tree branches were coated with white so that vertical black tree trunks seemed suspended in a cloud of white on the hillsides. The under story of small trees made layer upon layer of a snow lacework. The frozen pond was all white and buried under falling snow in grey/purple light. By nine AM, the sun was out in a blue sky as the cold front passed and during the morning break, I walked in the forest inside a white cloud, an infinity of horizontal white lines. Snow fell from a blue sunny sky as the wind blew it off the branches. Deer and rabbit tracks were everywhere in the new snow and a huge chorus of birdsong rang across the white landscape. I joined them, lost in the sparkling white and flashing diamonds of red, yellow, green. This is it! a voice in my head noted. Only this moment, right here, right now. All we have to do is let go of egos and grasping and there is the underlying perfection of existence.

At one AM of the last midnight practice of the Intensive Week, we all got a huge fresh-baked chocolate muffin and some tea. It was wonderful and I left a note of thanks to the cook, a young woman who was struggling harder than I was to keep going. The next morning she smiled and hugged me, and I suddenly realized that if you give happiness, you get happiness. Make people happy in small casual ways and you will be happy. Chocolate is not called *Theobroma* for nothing.

Zen Master Dae Kwang gave a talk at breakfast to mark the end of the intensive week.

"Zen means understanding yourself completely and then helping this world. Because we don't understand our true nature, we attach to passing desires and anger, like and dislike and create suffering for ourselves and others. Zen uses meditation to help us find our original nature before ego and thinking which is loving and compassionate. It means making your mind clear right now and then doing what you are doing without distracting thoughts. It is finding your true self and then helping this world. THAT IS ALL! But we always check to see what we get and what we didn't get – that is the mind of ego."

Listening, I cringed. That was exactly what I had been doing, trying to define some take-home lesson that would justify the time and effort.

"True Self says to come and do this retreat while thinking mind plots its escape," he continued. I cringed again. "We just have to keep putting one foot in front of the other and that will make a difference even though we don't perceive that in the midst of doing it. Zen practice is to keep clear mind and strong center, a total unwavering focus on doing practice in life, and then to help in whatever the situation is."

Walking in the snowy forest during a short break in the meditation schedule with only a sweater on, I realized that the thinking mind was finally becoming quieter and whenever it became quieter, I became happier. At the next purple dawn, a yellow full moon hung low over the Zen center drifting across the western sky. It seemed to float sideways as much as down and became a pink moon as the sky turned pink just before sunrise. Its drifting visible movement was time made visible, the earth's rotation made visible, the time of this retreat slowly drifting by. Wanting time to pass faster was like being a leaf on the Mississippi River. You move downstream at the rate the current is moving, you can't speed it up and you have no ability to move forward faster so you might as well relax. You will get there when the current gets you there. The morning's chanting and early sitting brought great joy and well-being for no particular reason. Was this a change in season or just a change in the daily mental weather? If this state were to persist, and develop over the next few weeks what a difference it would make.

All you get from kyol che is this moment and nothing else but the quality of this moment can change enormously. As the complaining mind weakens and we let go of internal mental chatter, life in each moment is more intense and gratitude, beauty and happiness arise. Walking to work, mist was pouring up off the woods and swamp in the morning sun, and small trees were covered with water droplets flashing in the sun. I didn't need a coat even though there was still a thin film of ice on the puddles. The geese were still on the half-thawed pond and that morning the dominant male ran off all but one female. The pair engaged in a little preliminary courtship, but by noon the rest of the flock was back. By the afternoon walk, it was sixty degrees.

The human world is marked by anger, ego, greed, ignorance and fighting. See any newspaper. Negative states seem to dominate over love and compassion in human affairs. If you want something that somebody else controls, no matter what or how small, be it a kong an answer, a certain status, an opportunity, that person controls you and there is no freedom. In a social setting the desire to be well liked, especially by somebody you already admire, arises instinctively. It keeps us from noticing the enormous beauty all around us that is visible in science, in rambling around in forest and sea and in moments of human kindness. We can still visit the Garden of Eden whenever we put down the apple of thinking.

At evening sitting a still mind appeared for a little while for the first time. It only took sixty-two days to have a moment of it arise!! At the

closing chants that night, I could actually chant them instead of enduring them. JOY, JOY! If this were to persist, what a breakthrough.

The seventieth day and the storm-tossed canoe was now over the mid-
continental shelf. A few gulls were visible. By the beginning of the next
to the last week, the canoe was over the inner continental shelf. The sea
was green not blue. A ship approaching land leaves relatively sterile clear
blue offshore water and moves into nutrient laden coastal water full of
microscopic green plankton. There was a faint line of land on the horizon.

At the next sitting enormous gratitude arose for all the wonderful
things in this life, especially gratitude for a situation that allowed me
the space for this retreat. All my life had been focused on achievement,
relationships and possessions – none of which survive death. Now it was
time to put some energy into what might survive death. Thinking stops
at death and what is left is only force of habit to guide the journey. Get
used to functioning that way and then at death, maybe there would be
no problem if the right mental habits were in place.

At the next interview, I brought up the mental squalls from pain,
fatigue etc.

"Why so much physical struggle? Why do we have to fight pain
instead of being quiet?"

"So you can practice not only when it is easy but also when it is hard.
In dying the body will have no energy at all and we need to practice then.
The body can be strong or weak but True Self is never changing."

"I wait the squalls out until they pass."

"There is no waiting something out, no getting through something,
no getting ready, no preparing and no closure," he said. "There is only this
moment. Just breathe really slowly. Keep clear mind and your demons
can't find you. Clear mind is non-chattering, non-thinking mind, and
demons are painful thoughts. They can't exist and cause pain unless they
are continuously recreated with thinking. Thinking is like a water faucet.
Turn it on when you need the water but when finished, turn it off. The
water faucet doesn't run 24/7."

When you realize that it is your own thinking making you miserable, realize that it is not just you. Nearly everybody has some sort of
major problem and thinks they would surely be happy if they could
just solve that problem. It may be a relationship, money, achievement,
physical ability or something else. But even if you solve that problem,

another one is sure to come along next. You can't control everything that happens or doesn't happen for you or to you, but you can control how your mind reacts to what happens or fails to happen. Happiness can only come from managing your thoughts and emotions. The mind is like a car. You have to learn to drive it carefully, not just hang on for the ride as it careens down the road. You don't get happiness, you make your happiness by how you manage your mind.

The brain's job is to identify and fix problems in life, but when we can't fix the problem, then we often start to obsess about it and make ourselves even more upset. Eventually life itself seems to be the problem. By all means, think about, analyze and try to solve your issue, but when you've done that, give it a rest. Don't keep going over it all again and again.

If you are dealing with a problem that you cannot fix or make go away, you have to change how you react to the situation mentally. Mental habits, repeated painful thoughts about a problem, keeps us from being happy. Start by realizing that these sorts of problems and disappointments are excellent teachers. They can teach valuable lessons, usually about things that we would never voluntarily try to learn, but since they are here, we might as well try to see what we can learn even as we keep trying to take actions to fix the problem. Eventually we can make new positive mental habits and create happiness for ourselves. We've been thinking a certain way for many years. We don't change those old mental habits overnight. It may take a long time and a lot of repeated efforts.

Every day we hiked in a silent line through the winter forest behind the monastery, climbing up and down the rocky ledges left behind as moraines by retreating Ice Age glaciers. Smaller rock outcrops were everywhere, buried in snow and dead leaves. I was overweight and had a weak knee so I always walked with my eyes glued to the unlevel ground in front of me, afraid of tripping and falling. One afternoon I tried to keep my eyes off the ground and walk more freely but it was impossible. In only a few weeks I had already created a strong new mental habit.

The worst mental habit is to keep reminding ourselves of what we don't have in life and at the same time failing to notice or be grateful for what we do have. STOP THAT!!!! Keep the mind focused on what is actually happening right now in this moment. We spend too much time worrying about how the future will turn out or regretting something in the past that cannot be changed now. Whenever the old repetitive obsessive thoughts about a problem appear, stop and see what is actually going on in this moment and pay attention to that, not to editorializing about the problem. If we are fully focused in the present, everything will go more smoothly in the present and then the future will turn out better than if we aren't doing our best right now.

Be consciously grateful for some small routine everyday thing that you have regardless of what else does or does not happen, something that you would usually just take for granted. Be grateful that you can breathe, walk across the room, see and hear. Appreciate the taste of food, the feeling of being rested or of getting out of a bath for example. We all have many such things. Notice what yours are and be grateful for just one thing each day.

When the mind really cuts loose with painful obsessive thinking and you can't stop it, just wait it out, knowing that it will eventually turn into thinking about something else. Endure it as you would endure a physical pain. Don't act out based on it while you are stuck in that pattern. Wait it out. While you are waiting it out, study it to see how it works and how it is making you unhappy. Treat your own unhappy mind as just something to observe and learn its tricks. Once you can see them, they can't control you as easily or make you quite as miserable. Find a way to give yourself something to break up the pattern. Do exercises, wash your face, sing a song or something like that.

If the problem involves a difficult relationship with another person or the desire to make a positive relationship with a new person: don't focus right away on what you want from the other person. Focus on "How can I make you happy? How can I help you?" If you want happiness, give happiness. Making somebody happy automatically makes you happy at the same time. On the other hand, if you send the message "I need help and I want you to help me" that makes you less attractive to the other person and they will be less likely to want to be involved with you. If you seem confident and at peace with yourself, you will be more attractive to the other person. This DOES NOT mean being on the receiving end of abusive or exploitive behavior. If the other person seems to be trying to take advantage of your effort to give rather than giving back in return, then be careful. Pay attention!

If someone is angry, it is your choice whether or not to respond with your own anger – if someone is hostile, don't take it personally but don't

allow yourself to be a victim either. Accept responsibility for your cir-
cumstances in life. Looking at what you have done to create the current
situation empowers you to do something differently rather than being a
passive victim

Pay attention to your thoughts and emotions as they arise – how does
it feel physically? Pay attention to self-talk, to how what you say to yourself reinforces the negative emotional state. Stop the negative speeches in
the head when they start. Consciously go and do something else. Think
about things that give you joy and gratitude. Don't keep repeating the
old painful stories you like to tell yourself about your problems. Peace
is how you are regardless of what is going on. It is not dependent on a
perfect situation because there is no perfect situation. It becomes just as
easy to replay the mental habit of joy as it is to replay the mental habit
of frustration and anger. The only total happiness comes from realizing
that your ego identity – your name, your body, your situation in life,
your strengths and weaknesses - is not who you really are. When you
realize what you really are then you can more easily deal with whatever
happens in day to day life – from a place of peace and wellbeing.

By the last week in March, the forest was incredibly alive. There
were two or three times as many song birds in the woods darting about
everywhere. Birds migrate in and out of the northern cold lands like
fish migrate in and out of an estuary, coming when conditions are good
and leaving when conditions become impossible. Pairs of migrating
ducks stopped over each night, dropping like rocks into the pond at the
last glimmer of light and leaving again at first daylight. If it weren't for
the long hours of the retreat schedule, nobody would have ever known
they were coming through. Big frogs, little spring peepers, kingfishers,
hawks, owls, squirrels, flying squirrels, chipmunks, deer, rabbits, coy-
otes, feral cats and turkeys were all over the place. How did those singing
adult frogs survive when the pond had been frozen solid? All the insects
appeared as soon as the temperature hit forty degrees. After all the snow
and ice, the sudden spring was like an explosion of life.

As the long-awaited end of the retreat began to appear on the horizon, doing this practice in a community became more important. I
finally even began to be grateful for mopping and vacuuming the floors.
There was housework here, there was housework at home. Housework
simply is, but here the mind got cleaned along with the floor. It was like

playing the piano or doing athletics. Once you grasp the principles then you have to practice it over and over until it is spontaneous and effortless, making new mental habits in the process. You don't get anything from practice except a different state of mind.

The last week and the headlands of that other shore were finally in sight! A few days before the retreat ended, little purple crocus flowers were blooming in a flower bed in front of the building. The only problem was the poem kong an. I had the entire fourth line except for one verb, but every verb that made any sense in the statement had already been rejected. It looked like I would have to leave without finishing it. To fail over one word was heartbreaking. After three months this kong an had lost all resemblance to the fluid spontaneous give-and-take that kong an practice was supposed to cultivate. I gave up the proper protocol of the interview room and asked to review all the rejected verbs I had tried, since I had probably forgotten to say it, but had written the right one down by mistake on the list of wrong answers I was secretly keeping. Since lived immediate non-verbal experience was the object of the retreat, keeping written notes about anything was not supposed to happen. My list was a total violation of the rules. The Zen Master looked a little startled when I pulled it out of my pocket, but bless his heart, he let me do it. He was probably as tired of the impasse as I was. And sure enough, there it was, one third of the way down the list after 103 failed verbs over 37 interviews. How many years to solve this kong an?

I celebrated the kong an solution by hiking in the woods after lunch.

"To all powers we call upon by all names, thank you for this kong an, thank you for this kyol che, for this forest, for this practice, for this life!" I prayed. I climbed up on one of the rocky outcrops and did a little dance and nearly fell off the cliff face. And laughed and laughed and laughed.

Every day of the last week, the sense of gratitude and joy became stronger and stronger. An old couple who had joined the retreat for a week were the same age as my husband and me. Watching them I was abruptly grateful for a lifelong good-hearted partner, friend and husband. Together we had built a tough but beautiful and meaningful life. I was grateful for all the support from so many other people that step by step had financed the years of education that allowed me to become a scientist and mentally thanked all of them. I was grateful for a warm spring day with butterflies and sitting with the doors to the meditation hall open. It was like a new lease on life. And all the friends and family at home. After evening sitting I went outside and looked at the growing April moon, the last full moon of the retreat. When I turned around to look at the stars in the darker part of the sky, a huge shooting star blazed across the sky like a response. I bowed.

The next morning I woke up grateful for the 4:30 AM wake up bell. It was the first time I ever welcomed that bell. It meant we were now only two days from the end and I finally knew I would actually complete kyol che after all. This retreat had been mostly about exploring unfinished business and partly about getting ready to die if necessary but it was more about learning how to live. At the last interview, I described the thank-you prayer and dance in the woods after the kong an answer and thanked Dae Kwang Sunim for all his help and teaching.

"Congratulations," he said and smiled. "Gratitude is a sign of a mature spiritual practice. And remember, the most interesting part of a long retreat is what happens afterward when you integrate back into daily life," he added.

Long-term meditation is like removing layer after layer of geological strata. On top are the affairs of daily life and all the thoughts and opinions about the personal situation. Take that off and it exposes old issues, old karma and mental habits that are influencing the surface from beneath. Sit a LONG time to resolve that and it may disappear. Then it is easier to perceive clearly, to know what to do with one's life moment to moment.

The retreat changed how I functioned mentally even if I didn't remember every insight or passing thought. Learning to see and manage the mind of dissatisfaction, I could really live in moment-to-moment clear mind. It changed the default emotional setting into one of great wellbeing. There was no "I" to manage the mind, it was just starting to function differently. The retreat was like wrapping a vine tendril around a fence so the vine would grow in a new direction. Twenty years practicing Zen. Leaving the temple on the last day, there was only a spring morning smell of wet earth along the roadside. Finally, it was enough.

CHAPTER 7

SEA TURTLES

When the rational, analytical mind
had done everything it could to ensure
catching a turtle, when the long silent
waiting began, we found ourselves
settling into the ancient mental state,
asking the turtle to come and allow itself
to be caught. And when it did, we gave
thanks for the gift of the turtle, tagged it
and sent it on its way with respect.

6:30 AM and our little turtle fishing boat raced into the Gulf of Mexico. It felt like the very first morning of the world, still sparkling fresh from creation. This day's fishing site was next to a huge oyster bar, several miles down the coast. We were trying to catch an Atlantic ridley, the most endangered species of sea turtle, to tag and release it. The Gulf coast is a place where these turtles grow up feasting on the abundance of blue crabs that live in the marshes, bays and grass beds. Fishing for turtles takes a lot of patience. We sat with the net for 12 hours, checking it every 30 minute to ensure that if a turtle got caught, it wouldn't drown before we got to it, A lot of days we didn't catch any at all. Most of the time was spent sitting and watching.

Turtles are everywhere, quietly and successfully bearing their shells through rock crevices, forests and deserts, ponds and lakes, and the high seas. Out of some 250 species of turtles, few have attracted more interest than the flippered behemoths that swim the world's vast oceans. Between them, the handful of species of modern sea turtles have adapted to nearly every available marine environment. Most seem to share a drifting life on the high seas as babies, foraging for their first several years in food rich areas called convergence zones where currents come together and sargassum weed and other drifting material concentrates. When they outgrow that food supply, they then move inshore to take up the specialized life style of their own species.

Elegant green sea turtles graze tropical undersea meadows of sea grass, while enormous leatherbacks weighing some 1500 pounds dive thousands of feet into the black frigid depths to harvest jellyfish, routinely accessing a world that is almost beyond human reach. Kemp's ridleys hunt crabs in a foot of muddy water around coastal oyster bars. Heavy yellow loggerheads hunt horseshoe crabs and crush snails along temperate continental shelves while olive ridleys ride the waves of the open ocean, sunning hundreds of miles from land, providing a perch for a bird. Hawksbills patrol the sunlit tropical shallows around coral reefs, one of the few species to ever master the art of eating sponges.

Along with black turtles and Australian flatbacks, all of them must obey biological laws. As air breathing reptiles descended from terrestrial ancestors, they lay shelled eggs. That keeps them tied to the land as females emerge periodically from the sea onto tropical and subtropical beaches to lay their eggs. The coast that builds a suitable nesting beach may be thousands of miles from the feeding grounds, and as a result, sea turtles engage in high seas migrations of enormous distance with individuals homing to the same spot year after year, often after journeys of thousands of miles. Their breeding habits are as diverse as their feeding styles. Hawksbills stampede across brushy rocky scraps of sand to nest secretively under seaside bushes and trees while thousands of olive ridleys storm ashore in a single night in mass nestings called arribadas. As they go about their affairs, sea turtles provide scientists with endless challenges. Big fast ocean ranging animals are just plain hard to study in the field and after years of intensive effort, we still know very little about them. And turtles, like dragons, are important cultural symbols in Asia. The ancient Chinese divination system called the I Ching originally used cracks in turtle shells to give seekers advice and answer their questions.

Waves slapped on the bow of our boat as we pulled along the top of the turtle net. If we caught one of these small sea turtles, it would be tagged and released. Where they go, how long they live, how they find their way from one widely scattered spot to another - only the fewest of facts are known. And aside from the scientific challenge, our lack of understanding of sea turtles posed a danger to their continued survival. When a turtle was captured with a tag in its flipper, it would tell us something of how young turtles use the marshes and grass beds, how fast they grow, how long they stay around — details that might help to preserve it from extinction.

Everywhere they go, sea turtles are in the way of somebody or they are part of somebody's dinner plans. From ongoing direct harvest of meat and eggs to accidental drowning in fishing gear, from the habitat destruction when a dark isolated breeding beach is built into an expensive seaside resort to choking on the ever increasing amount of plastic garbage in the sea - they have died in innumerable ways at human hands.

Preventing extinction is becoming one of the primary issues in ecology today. This green and blue planet, shining in the sunshine, is the only one we know to be alive. That life is divided up into millions of species, so many that after centuries of work we still don't have accurate count. It has been ruthlessly pruned back in repeated mass extinctions in the past. The most severe, approximately 230 million years ago, is estimated to have resulted in the loss of 75 to 90 percent of all species on earth. Eventually, after millions of years, the survivors rediversify and new species fill the vacancies.

Millions of years after we're gone, the planet will heal itself, but that's not what the argument is about. The issue is really about us, what kind of world we want for ourselves and our grandchildren and their grandchildren. Will we leave them their full heritage of living beauty of this planet? Even if we assume that these myriads of other species must be judged only by their usefulness or lack of it to humans, do we know enough to decide what's worth keeping? The total number of species may be some 3 million. But some estimates put it closer to 30 million. Three or thirty? If we don't even know that, how can we possibly pretend to understand how the planet works, which species are essential and which aren't? About half of all drugs used in medicine were derived initially from wild plants and animals. Recent screening of other species has yielded drugs that treat cancer, encephalitis, arteriosclerosis, blood pressure problems, dysentery. We haven't even screened 1 percent of the species available, yet each is a potential source of new and unique life-saving medicines.

The falling tide raced around the end of the bar and in the calm lee small fish called menhaden swirled in huge schools, looking like moving patches of raindrops hitting the water. Hundreds of gulls, cormorants, terns and pelicans wheeled and screamed, feeding on the concentrated fish. The frantic swarming of menhaden and birds lasted for about an hour until the falling tide scattered the fish schools further offshore. The morning continued to turn, the sun rose higher in the sky and the sea and marsh were silent under the weight of the heat and the glare.

By noon the sea grass began to be exposed on the tide flats. Then the place came to life again, this time with mullet. The mirror surface of the grass-streaked shallows was broken into splashes and ripples as the big fish rolled and fed. Ten to 12 ospreys hovered overhead, dropping from the sky like arrows to seize a mullet. When it was time to check the net, we pulled our skiff along the cork line of the net by hand, lifting it up, looking for the flash of white in the murky water that meant either a ray, a shark or a turtle. The mesh was so big that anything smaller passed through. If it was a shark or a ray we released it. Although the turtle population was beginning a slow recovery from decades of egg harvest and drowning in nets, most of the time the net was empty, and I realized in a way I never did before that this once common sea turtle really was close to extinction.

Native American hunters, when they stalked game, had a wealth of knowledge of the animals' habits, which they used to track the game effectively. But they did more. A hunt was often preceded by a period of meditation and purification, and in the hunt they tried to merge themselves with the world, to let the animal know the hunter's need. Then it would come and allow itself to be taken so that the people might continue to live. The hunter and the hunted were bound together in mutual relationship and respect.

Similarly, we had chosen the most likely tide, had built a net that would catch turtles efficiently, and talked to other fishermen about where they'd spotted turtles. But when the rational, analytical mind had done everything it could to ensure catching a turtle, when the long silent waiting began, we found ourselves settling into the ancient mental state, asking the turtle to come and allow itself to be caught. And when it did, we gave thanks for the gift of the turtle, tagged it and sent it on its way with respect.

Zen Master Man Gong once gave a speech at the end of a three month Zen retreat.

"All of you sat in the dharma room (meditation hall) for three months. That is very, very wonderful! As for me, I only stayed in my room making a net. This net is made from special string. It is very strong and can catch Buddha, Dharma, Bodhisattvas, human beings, everything. How do you get out of this net?"

Some students shouted or hit the floor or raised a fist, all typical Zen style gestures. One said "Already got out. How are you, Zen Master?" Another said, "Don't make net." To all these responses Man Gong only answered, "Aha! I've caught another big fish!"

Zen nets catch more than fish or turtles. Dogen, the founder of the Japanese Soto Zen tradition, once said, "From ancient times wise people and sages lived near water. When they live near water, they catch fish, catch human beings, and catch the Way. For long these have been genuine activities in water. Furthermore, there is catching the self, catching catching, being caught by catching and being caught by the Way."

That giving of thanks for catching the turtle was highly unorthodox in a scientific research project. In science only matter and energy are real and human consciousness is generally assumed to be a random byproduct of neural complexity. We can survive better with expanded awareness, so mind is merely a result of natural selection. Subjective mental phenomena, both ordinary consciousness and alternative states of consciousness, are excluded from consideration. Questions about any meaning of human life are irrelevant and ignored. Materialism is usually presented as an integral part of science. To do otherwise raises the specter of religious dogma once again controlling scientific research as it did in Galileo's day.

For 500 years scientific investigation has focused on a reductionist approach, dissecting systems into their components in order to understand the whole by a complete description of the parts. Using it, we have learned more about nature than in all of previous human history combined, but reductionism is limited in its ability to describe, model or predict the complex forms and organizations that dominate nature

In 1983, the mathematician Benoit Mandelbrot described fractal mathematics that for the first time allowed the quantitative description of complex natural shapes and opened up the scientific study of how complex systems can spontaneously emerge out of simpler ones. When the simple equations of fractal mathematics are repeated with each set of results becoming the starting values for the next repetition, the calculation produces patterns of enormous complexity that are self-similar at all scales of size and are never exactly alike. They reproduce the forms of natural structures, both living and nonliving, such as a coastline or clouds or a network of blood vessels. Fractal patterns in nature range from the distribution of galaxies in space to microscopic biological tissues. Humans in crowds form fractal patterns. The lights of small towns seen from a jet window at night sometimes form fractal patterns. Thunderstorms, the beating of the heart, the firing of neurons, the behavior of the stock market, the shape of a flock of birds or a school of fish, trees and the human brain have fractal characteristics. A vortex spinning off of a canoe paddle, a devastating tornado that drops out of a thunderstorm, these highly structured patterns seem to have an independent existence but they are only a pattern of organization that persists momentarily in the larger stream.

Complex systems characterized by fractal patterns are endlessly creative. Physical and biological systems that have irregular fractal shapes are self-organizing, generating emergent complexity that could not be predicted in advance from analyzing their components and thus are endlessly evolving and creating new details. The tiniest differences in initial conditions in these nonlinear systems result in hugely different outcomes as they evolve as well as abrupt shifts from one state to the next. Fundamental laws govern the process but the details of what arises are unpredictable, constantly generating new diversity.

Darwinian natural selection of random mutations, while quite real and powerful to the evolution of life, may not alone be sufficient to account for the evolution of the biological diversity that we observe around us. While present, it may not be the whole story. The universe is intrinsically creative and unpredictable, with the continual evolution of new forms built into its deepest fabric. The emergence of complex living forms and of consciousness itself arises from the inherent nature of the fractal self-organizing universe. With the paradigm of complexity theory, we may someday begin to comprehend the most complex self-organizing systems that occur in biology, perhaps even how consciousness emerges from biological systems. Complexity theory and fractal mathematics do not replace or supplant Newton's laws or biological evolution through natural selection, they supplement and extend them. They better explain the creativity of the universe and the evolution of new forms than the more static Newtonian clockwork universe view alone.

The history of life written in the fossil record is an explosion of ever increasing diversity. If dinosaurs had not disappeared, then giraffes, cats and human beings would probably never have arisen. The birth and death of human beings endlessly produces unique new minds and consciousness, new insights and talents. If we didn't die and replace the last generation with the next generation, human innovation would probably disappear. If Mozart didn't have to die, Stravinsky could not have been born. It is possible to let go of personal fear and to perceive the brilliance of the process and to know that one's approaching death is part of a vaster and extraordinary reality.

Each of us is part of a fractal universe in which we see the repetition of its most fundamental patterns of organization at all scales of size. A fractal system, like the universe in which we live, is self-similar at all scales of size. The existence of larger scale transcendent Mind is not only possible but would even be probable in a fractal self-organized universe that is self-similar at all scales. Consciousness at our level of scale means there should be something very similar at larger and smaller scales as well in a fractal universe. The ability of individuals to interact with a larger scale Mind becomes possible because we and it are all aspects of one integrated whole. The same dynamics that formed the mountains are the dynamics that formed my individual consciousness. The poet William Blake said "to see the world in a grain of sand and eternity in an hour." Fractal self-similarity makes this literally true. We don't come into the universe; we come out of the universe.

Our turtle net made swirls in the water as we pulled it for the last time at sunset. The swirls were fractal. Complexity theory and the recognition that quantum effects are acting in macroscopic living systems are relatively new perspectives in science but they are consistent with very old ideas in mystical religion, especially in Buddhism. The ancient Buddhist observation that all things are impermanent is a direct consequence of the fact that the universe is a chaotic fractal system that is ever changing and dynamic. Complexity theory could be considered to be a scientific formulation of the ancient Buddhist concept of interdependence, the interdependent co origination and interbeing of all things, the lack of completely independent self-existence apart from everything else. In Buddhism Nothingness is the fertile generative creative source of all things. The parallel between this term and physicists' description of a vacuum from which sub atomic particles suddenly emerge is interesting to say the least. The two disciplines are not necessarily describing the same phenomenon, but they may be complementary approaches to exploring the unknown that can inform each other. For the first time in centuries, quantum mechanics and complexity theory are pushing the two worlds of mind and matter, of science and the creative explosions of form that have always been the subject of religion, a little closer together.

While theoretical models are intriguing, hands on field science and getting wet and dirty was where I preferred to be. A few weeks later, the last yellow glow of sunset silhouetted a dwarf cypress forest, while to the east a full moon sailed past windblown thunderheads that blasted the land beneath them with bolt after bolt of lightning. It was so far away that the light show was silent. This huge place called the Everglades seemed remote but it was only a few minutes' drive from the Miami airport. Big as it was - some 1.5 million acres of saw grass, mangrove and Florida Bay sea grasses full of birds, fish and sea turtles -- it was all at the edge of the urban east coast. Its water flow was stolen to sustain that world of freeways, pavement, trucks and incessantly roaring air conditioners as well as vast sugar cane fields on the edge of the Everglades. Year by year, its birds and sea grass were disappearing.

Big as it was, the Everglades wasn't big enough, but it was still the sort of place that one expects to see a green sea turtle. While green turtles have been studied for years on their breeding beaches, far less is known of green turtles at sea. In Everglades National Park, a team of scientists caught and tagged the green and loggerhead sea turtles that foraged in the vast sea grass beds of south Florida waters. I had been invited to join the research team for a weekend of field work tagging and describing the Everglades sea turtles and jumped at the chance. It was a different world from the muddy North Florida estuaries where Jack and I did research on the Kemp's ridley sea turtle.

The largest of the hard shelled sea turtles, adult greens may weigh 300 or more pounds. The heart shaped shell is a sunburst pattern of brown, tan, greenish and black above a yellowish to whitish belly shell. Once they nested throughout the Caribbean - Bermuda, Cuba, Barbados, the Florida Keys and so on. In US waters they occurred as far north as North Carolina in the summer. Large adults occurred around the Cedar Keys of the northern Gulf coast just south of our aquarium.

The next morning, in the vivid slanting light just after sunrise, our three boat flotilla raced into the maze of mangrove islands and shallow sea grass flats that is Florida Bay, between the Everglades and the Florida

Keys to the south. Eventually the boats stopped and the team of scientists set a net out hand over hand, shaking out the tangles. In addition to greens, adult male and female loggerheads were common, and there were at least 5 of them around the boat. Loggerheads stayed in the deep tidal channel, while small greens were in the shallows on the grass flat. Turtle heads popped up and down all over the flat.

"The boat's here, the net is there and that turtle is right in the middle," moaned one of the biologists. A green turtle blew in front of us and then another behind the boat. A loggerhead sat at the surface several hundred feet off the bow but the net floats remained motionless. It was a tiny piece of net in a vast bay. Seeing a turtle is one thing, catching it is another.

A green turtle surfaced 50 feet away. "Come on over here," everybody called but it wasn't buying. A loggerhead swam up to the boat, the huge head rising vertically above the water, just out of reach. The jon boat crew worked its way down the net checking it, pulling themselves hand over hand. Empty. By then 7 turtles were running circles around the net as wind and chop picked up and a tide flat went dry behind us. Thunder rolled. Moments of breathtaking beauty flashed on and off as the world was glittering gold and purple one instant and dull grey and windy the next. Clouds and sun waltzed round and round each other as turtles waltzed around us and our tiny net. The turtles were in charge here, eluding the nets effortlessly.

The sea grasses beneath our hulls were flowering plants derived from terrestrial ancestors. They flower and set seed just as do oats or daises but they do it underwater, with currents rather than wind or insects to scatter their seed. Named for the green turtles that eat it, the most abundant of these grasses in the Caribbean is turtle grass which, depending on the depth to which light penetrates the sea, can grow from just below the low tide mark to a depth of 100 or more feet. Shoal grass, manatee grass, and star grass grow in association with turtle grass, each species in its own preferred depth. It's easy to tell if green sea turtles are foraging by their characteristic cropping marks on the plants. They prefer fresh shoots over tall older blades of grass and maintain patches of closely cropped blades, underwater gardens, to which they return repeatedly. They like large contiguous pastures and stay in deeper areas, using both clear and turbid water areas. Greens also feed heavily on red algae in some areas.

A green turtle surfaced by the channel marker 100 feet past the net. And another surfaced again next to the anchored empty 3rd boat. Eventually the crew gave up on the net, pulled it and moved to another area where the water was clear enough for diving.

They put sleds over and towed 2 divers. Two divers sat on the bow of one of the other skiffs, poised to jump if they got close enough to a turtle. In their body language, they were the direct descendants of whaling harpooners. Suddenly one of them peeled off to the left chasing a turtle. Both boats converged, but the turtle escaped.

In their black wetsuits, the divers swam in formation above the thick grassy carpet below our hulls. Ashore a sea of saw grass had scattered tree islands, but out here in the bay mangrove islands were scattered across an ocean meadow of turtle grass. This meadow had salt water over it, not air, and that made all the difference in what could live there.

The hunt continued with minds focused and alert, eyes scanning the surface of the sea for the swirl of a surfacing turtle out here on the foraging grounds where the turtles actually live their lives. Hunting, hunting, the biologists spotted another turtle and the divers chased it in a relay system. As one diver tired, a fresh swimmer from the boat would replace him and so on until the turtle tired enough to be grabbed. After a while it quit running and started to dodge back and forth.

"It's a game," said one scientist over the roar of the outboard motor. "to figure out where it will surface next and go there. Which way is it headed, which way is the current running? A green just rockets off in one direction but if you can see a loggerhead underwater there's a pretty good chance you can catch it. They can outswim you but they have trouble deciding which way to go. They go one way and then turn around and come back again. They're good at making bad decisions," she laughed. "You stay with them until you can get close."

"There he is straight ahead! Go! Go! Go!" she suddenly yelled. The two in the water both dropped their tow boards and took off like a pair of hunting porpoises after a school of mullet - looking big and predatory, purposeful and dangerous cutting through the water. Then the human predators were circling over the turtle, closing in for the capture. The turtle turned in tighter and tighter circles, and then they all dove. Three heads appeared together in a bobbing cluster at the surface, two human, and one green turtle. As soon as the hunt was over, the processing began.

The turtle joined the human world, got a name -Tag Left:X 2176;Tag Right:BP2477. It took 4 people to flip it over onto its back to get the belly shell or plastron measurements, everybody dodging the flailing flippers that could easily knock somebody onto the deck. That turtle tagged and released, we resumed the hunt.

Suddenly a diver let go of his tow and by the time we turned the boat around, he was at the surface with a young green that had been tucked under a rock ledge. With a snowy white belly and brown and black and tan sunrises on the shell, its colors were bright, vivid and well defined. The skin around the neck and shoulders was bright yellow and black. It was a beautiful little creature, fat and perfect.

Schools of scallops swam away from our bow wake. At first I thought they were some kind of baby flounders. It took a second to realize that scallops could be that abundant. Out there in the seemingly endless turtle pastures of the sea where turtles were as abundant as they ought to be, all was right with the world. All the environmental worries of modern ecologists were also far away. Maybe the human race would be ok too. It was hard to believe otherwise in that moment. A Zen paradox says "Everything is perfect, just the way it is." In that moment it was unquestionably true.

As we returned to port that night, a Zen poem came to mind:

Ten thousand fishing lines
Straight down.
      One wave
Becomes ten thousand waves.
Darkness and cold water.
The fish aren't biting tonight.
The empty ship returns
Full of moonlight.

DANCING IN THE VALLEY
OF THE SHADOW

Coming empty handed, going empty
handed – that is human. When you are
born, where do you come from? When
you die, where do you go? Life is like a
floating cloud that appears. Death is
like a floating cloud that disappears. The
floating cloud originally does not exist.
Life and death, coming and going, are
also like that. But there is one thing that
always remains clear. It is pure and clear,
not depending on life and death. What is
that one pure and clear thing?

The Human Route (Zen poem)

My eyes blinked open as consciousness returned after the colonoscopy. Before I could say anything, the doctor leaned over my shoulder and said in an urgent voice, "You have cancer!"

"Geez, what kind of a bedside manner is that?" I thought in a fuzzy blur. A few hours before, when I had arrived at the clinic for a routine screening, I had felt fine. It was just the last step in a series of routine checkups.

"But you'll be O.k.," he added. "It's small, we think we caught it before it spread beyond the gut."

But it had spread. And after surgery to remove the tumor and a series of lymph nodes, I spent weeks recovering under huge old trees next to the Gulf of Mexico in the company of fall wildflowers and butterflies. Morning sunlight glittered on the bay and gilded the pine needles overhead. I was swept not with fear but with gratitude for all the wonderful things of life and with the absolute conviction that, if death came, nothing would be lost.

Later, my husband and I made a trip to the Moffitt Cancer Center in Tampa. On the way, we canoed the Weeki Wachee River, a gorgeous spring run with crystal clear water, underwater emerald meadows, schools of fish darting past us, manatees and eagles. The healing that came from being there was palpable, even as it had been under the pines at home. There was joy to be a part of a system that creates such beauty even though death is part of it.

Halfway through the initial chemotherapy, I ended up in and out of the hospital over 25 days, really sick. I never felt as if I were in any serious danger, given that medical support was available but a lot of friends who saw me were convinced that I was on the brink of death and the doctors didn't say that it was out of the question.

Neighbors came to visit and they always wanted to pray. I welcomed the kindness even if the language was not the same as I was used to in my own religious practice. This culminated in the appearance in my front yard one Sunday afternoon after I got out of the hospital of about 20 members of a little lay led church. Everybody gathered around my husband and me, but in the little village of Panacea, where neighbors still know each other, it was well known that neither my husband nor I was an orthodox believer. They were a little uncertain about how to begin with a couple of lost souls, one of whom might be facing an early death.

I began by thanking them for their care and all the covered dinners and they began to share the value of their faith. I found that I truly agreed with everything that was said, with the exception that theirs was the only way. Then I said that the most mistaken thing anybody can say in this situation is "Why me?" because sooner or later we must all face this sort of trouble and eventually we will all die of something. Rather, I said, a health crisis is a wonderful teacher if we can let go of anger and fear and open up to what it has to teach.

The preacher immediately added, "We should give thanks for cancer because it brings us closer to God and that is the most important thing in life." He then turned and looked at the other members of his congregation. Nodding at individuals one by one, he said, "And you should give thanks for the breast cancer," and you, nodding to another, "mental illness, and you," nodding to another, "should give thanks for that shooting, " and you, nodding to another, "for the heart attack." Everyone he pointed to agreed.

So, was he right? Should we not only be brave but even thankful if we get cancer? I reflected on my own case and realized that the preacher was right.

After six years of treatment, I learned to live with a deep seated sense of 'only don't know, go straight," as our founding Zen Master loved to say. To fully know what it is to be human, it is just as important to go through the hard times of old age, loss of social roles, illness and approaching death as to go through the more pleasant phases of youth. It's all part of seeing things as they truly are. If all the hard stuff could be avoided, it would be only a half view of what a human life actually is. The hard parts provide unique insight and wisdom if one is open to the experience.

Getting the unexpected news of a major health crisis when you haven't felt sick or thought much about such things is a huge shock for many people. The mind may go numb. We search the hardest for meaning when sickness, tragedy, loss and death come. No matter how life changes, it is a given that there will be some challenge before us to deal with. It is important to do everything needed to deal with the situation as well as possible medically and emotionally, but once that is in place, there is no need to let it take over every minute of your life.

Sometimes the only part of a situation that is in our control is the state of our own mind. Is it patient and peaceful or is it frightened and angry? Eventually meditation became a prayer for mental clarity and strength. In my experience, that prayer had always been answered.

Keeping the mind in the present moment and minimizing self-centered abstract thought leads to wellbeing because self-centered thought is where the negativity lives. There is a lot we can do to better manage the mind, so that it helps us to be at peace with the way things turn out regardless of whether that result was what we wanted or not what we wanted. Try to solve problems but at the same time don't let the mind add more mental suffering with obsessive thinking on top of what is already going on. It makes all the difference in the world in experiencing life as the gift that it is.

Cancer can appear out of nowhere and sweep someone away in a few months or it can be a slow-moving process of alternating sickness and stability, unfolding over several years. For those with a possibility of either a cure or a fatal recurrence, there is living with perpetual uncertainty. The knowledge that time may be limited creates a new sense of urgency about finally doing what has been put on hold year after year.

Any personal crisis like a potentially fatal cancer diagnosis or a heart attack may trigger a lot of fundamental questions about meaning as well as reflection and a review of one's life. For many of us, the mind wanders to trying to make sense of this life. What am I? What is life and death all about? When we die, what happens? Is there some ultimate purpose or meaning to our lives, to being conscious? Is there some ultimate reason for the existence of complex organisms and consciousness and what could it be? How can I do better? These are the most important questions in life but most of the time, we stay lost in the endless affairs of daily life. It is primarily in times of crisis that we stop and struggle with the big questions. If we are open to exploring, they can be the great gift of such challenges.

The most defining characteristic of an individual life is that it is a short finite experience proceeding inexorably through all its stages from infancy to old age and then out. The individual personality is literally as fleeting as a star at dawn, a bubble in a stream, a flash of lightning in a summer cloud, a flickering lamp, a phantom and a dream, in the poetic words of the Diamond Sutra. It seems remote in youth but as we age, this truth becomes more and more immediate. Midges dancing in the afternoon sunlight, totally focused on their affairs, are not so different from people buzzing about taking care of business.

As the Buddha pointed out thousands of years ago, we create tragedy and loss by being attached to things or beings that are intrinsically impermanent including our health, our wealth and each other. Thinking that we are limited to our physical bodies and brains, we fear death and the separation from that which we love. We see death as an extinction of being that we strive to postpone as long as possible because we fear that consciousness is created only by the physical brain and must therefore cease when the brain dies. Contemporary medicine often prolongs life too long because of that fear.

Even though an impermanent brief life is a defining characteristic of the human experience, most of us are in denial of this and shut it out as long as possible rather than asking what is the point of a life that will soon stop. Nobody really believes that it will happen to them until it does. Why do we want some part of personal consciousness to survive? Who is it that wants survival so badly? What exactly is it that is wanted? Nobody has yet succeeded in settling these questions once and for all despite everyone's efforts for thousands of generations. Finding joy in the midst of the storm is one of the most beneficial things we can do for ourselves. We have to relearn how to really live fully in the present, how to live happily here and now.

Finding meaning in life may become the overwhelming task of this phase of life in between medical procedures. The great matter of life and death comes into the forefront of the mind. God is usually conceived in western religion as a giant King and Creator who made and rules the universe. When we cry out for help and when help appears, we say that God answered the prayer and assume it must be this sort of Creator deity. However, perhaps what we refer to as God is not a separate CEO or King or Creator apart from the creation. God could be the transcendent large-scale consciousness of a universe which is literally alive and conscious, self-emergent, self-sustaining, self-fulfilling. While there is no separate mover apart from that which is moved in this model, the entire movement is sentient and compassionate and responsive.

If the religious mystics who say the universe is interactive, responding to us, molding itself around us in some way, are right, such an intrinsic large-scale awareness might respond to prayer from its individual component minds just as an immune system responds to the needs of its parts. When a part of the physical body is injured, signals are sent into the entire body and the immune system, which is an integral part of the same body as the injured part, responds. The injured part and the responding immune system are not separate and the response is already built into the very fabric of the organism.

When somebody dies, it means that a personality disappears from the network of social relationships that includes our own personality and that of others. We mistakenly think that the personality that died was a distinct separate being even though it makes no sense that it appeared out of nothing and then becomes nothing. The labeling of life-times and consciousness into distinct individual beings, while it is not totally wrong, greatly exaggerates and overemphasizes our sense of isolation and impermanence. Much of the fear and suffering that surrounds death comes from our ignorance that what we are may transcend the physical body.

Individual personalities resemble tiny eddies in a swirling ocean of sentience. Life and death might be only a transformation and no problem. In this model, consciousness would not be a constant unchanging entity called a soul, but an ever-changing fluid event in which birthdays and death days are arbitrary waypoints, artificial constructs imposed on the process of birth, growth, aging and death.

Does an individual eddy merge into an ocean? There's no point in speculating with imagery like this. Reviewing the events of one's life, trying to find some point to it, is looking at the wrong scale. Every one of billions and billions of human lives are a series of details and events that arise over and over but nobody has ever resolved an ultimate meaning to the phenomenon of life or consciousness from all those individual biographies.

In thousands of species of animals related to jellyfish, the swimming jellyfish stage gives rise to an anchored plant-shaped colonial animal and it in turn produces more jellyfish. Unlike the solid anchored polyp, the transparent delicate swimming medusa is barely separate from the water in which it moves. The swimming jellyfish and the anchored colonial stage cycle endlessly in a process called alternation of generations.

If some part of consciousness should survive the death of the brain, as all the world's religions claim, is it simply the launching of a jellyfish into the open ocean, of a vastness swept by currents that are inconceivable to the stage which is firmly rooted on its rock? Perhaps life and death are simply the alternation of generations of consciousness between a brained-based material state and a nonmaterial state and our lives are only a piece of a larger cycle that is completed by a death-to-birth segment. If there is an alternation of generations of consciousness between a brained-based material state and a nonmaterial state, what we call supernatural will turn out to be as biological as any other aspect of life. There's nothing paranormal or magic. The immaterial is just an unexplained aspect of nature that we have yet to know with the science of the material state.

If we could know that death is not final, that it is more of a transition than an ending, then dying per se would not be so frightening, Much of the seeming cruelty and indifference of nature's endless life and death would become much less of an issue. Mortality and the impermanence of an individual lifetime, while very real, become a wonderful aspect of reality. Death becomes a source of creativity and beauty of nature. Most people do not agree with the Buddhist teaching that being born is already a mistake, but people coming out of near-death experiences are often angry to be resuscitated.

Death might not mean giving up the beauty of life. It might only mean a better view of the larger wonders of the universe. We can learn to face death with equanimity and even curiosity for the adventure. The body's decay may prove to be no more significant than the hair we leave behind on the floor of the barbershop.

Positive things are no longer taken for granted. Getting upset about the smaller stresses of daily life can be greatly reduced. What used to be big problems are no longer that important relative to the possible closing out of a lifetime in the near future. Life can be much less cluttered with personal problems. Facing the ultimate questions of meaning in life can allow us to really drop the ego-based worries over career and finances that often drive us nuts for years, to let go of stuff that is exhausting and to replace it with things we really want to do. And the sky does not fall as a result of these changes. We can actually enjoy each day a lot more.

Any major illness means one really must live in the present moment rather than being lost in the past or in fearful or desire-ridden fantasies of the future. It is important to do everything needed to deal with the situation as well as possible medically and emotionally, but once that is in place, there is no need to wallow in the center of an emotional self-centered melodrama. If there is health and energy in a given moment, one can live it fully and not take it for granted or destroy it by fear of what may lie in the future. There's no need to turn healthy moments into sickness with mental stress. In a prolonged slow-moving challenge like a potentially terminal illness, we can use this different quieter time to find a new source of significance for this life, something that is not up to others to give or withhold. Then we can do what projects we undertake without being upset at how they turn out when there are difficulties. There will be an internal restructuring as well as an external restructuring of daily life.

Millions of people are going through similar challenges. All over the world people work hard to kill each other in wars every day and thousands die in natural disasters and accidents. They were not statistics or news stories, they were individual people who hoped and loved and worried about life. Against this background it is neurotic self-absorption to obsess about one possible death in particular – namely our own. We will all die sooner or later, one way or another. Rather than making such a production about it, just do what's needed in this moment. It is important to develop a personally meaningful view of life now since if we wait until the end, there may not be the time or energy to do it at the last minute.

Life is not just about what we know, it's about how we are and what we are doing. The job of this life is to live this life fully, intensely and focused in the here-and-now rather than endlessly wondering about what may come at the time of death. A life should be lived so that it is not defined by when one dies. It will unfold according to its own inner timing. There is no need to try to force things in a rigid goal-seeking way.

Along with facing life and death, the second core question of spiritual practice is whether or not all the stuff we do in life has some transcendent significance. Is a lifetime what I will it to be or is it just what appears before me? Is there really some cosmic assignment for a lifetime? We can invent a Great Work, convince ourselves that that is what we are alive to do and then become deeply frustrated when it doesn't work out according to plan. If our wellbeing depends in part on a sense that life has a meaning and we think we know what that meaning is but can't quite achieve it, then it becomes just another source of suffering as a result of trying to enforce a rigid control over a complex dynamic evolving situation.

There is no need to worry about exactly how life unfolds or to be frustrated at unaccomplished things. The Great Work of a lifetime is an evolving event that can only be known as it arises and will only become clear at the end of a lifetime as what it turned out to be. Do not try to arbitrarily squeeze that creative unpredictable process down into some rigid narrow definition of what it ought to be and then wall off and resist what it in fact is.

Controlling how life unfolds is not possible. Instead of falling into that trap, we can apply the same insight to our individual lives that applies to the rest of the universe: that it's a dynamic evolving creative system, that it is intrinsically unpredictable and uncontrollable, but that unpredictability and uncontrollability are the essential source of the creativity that keeps life dynamic and full of discovery.

What may happen at death is interesting but the more accessible aspect of the effort is learning how to really live fully in the present, how to live happily here and now. How much we achieve and how well we are known is not as important as how much we experience and what level of awareness and insight come out of the experience. What we do is more important than what we think because doing is what gives structure to the day, to how we actually live the moments of our lives.

No matter how life changes, it is a given that there will be some challenge before us to deal with. The mind makes exhaustion and sorrow, but it also makes energy and joy. Keeping the mind centered and focused on what is actually happening moment to moment is the keel that keeps the boat stable in smooth or rough water. Make your best effort in each moment but then be open to whatever arises in the next moment. This can only be done if we are not trying to get some particular result and if we know how to simply watch the mind and recognize when it engages in a painful thought process. Take care of the present moment and the future will take care of itself. Cultivating this state of mind is the one and only thing that we will never lose. Clearly see the processes of the ego-mind when it is acting so that it is our servant, not our master, and live in a way that is conducive to the arising of the alternative moment-to-moment mental state of Being. Life is hard but also fine and beautiful. It is unpredictable and short but it is also wonderful. Mind makes everything. If you make hell with your thinking, you get hell, but if you make heaven with thinking, you get heaven. Only cease to cherish your opinions and then you will get everything someday or maybe right now in this moment.

Live life as a Great Question, as an endless open ended exploration of an evolving event. Have the Great Courage to not lock down life's meaning into some rigid idea but to continue the open-ended exploration. And keep Great Faith, that a resolution is possible. Moments of altered mental states are traditionally emphasized as a major goal of a spiritual practice, but the fruits of those moments as they inform daily life are more important than waiting for another such moment.

The most important mental habit to cultivate is "enough mind," the sense that all is truly well in this moment. Having an awake and actualized life is not only the memory of some special moment when the mind opened to some degree. It also consists of how we are moment to moment right now, of being fully awake and aware and of being responsive in each moment one after the other and of a mind that is informed by compassion to help and of knowing the sources of suffering in the specific situation at hand.

Do I keep a mind totally focused in the present and free of self-centered suffering or do I not? The simpler life is, the easier it is to reinforce the habit of keeping a still clear mind. It is a practice to be done daily just like sitting on a meditation cushion or prayer. It is the moment-to-moment practice of being alert, calm, clear and ready to respond to the situation spontaneously as it develops, without having to figure it out. That mental state can be there in one minute and not the next.

Joyfulness comes from appreciation and gratitude for all the wonderful details that were being overlooked before. Joy comes from being aware and appreciating, from being grateful for what is. Painful thought patterns can't exist and can't cause pain unless we endlessly recreate them with thinking.

Understanding how to live this way is only conceptual understanding. Being lost in abstract thought means you are not actually doing it. It is a necessary starting point but attaining means having the actual personal experience of it. Actualizing that experience means actually living out of it, acting in some way that manifests it in the world, doing something rather than just thinking about it. First notice and understand; then attain and then manifest it, doing something in this life to actualize awareness. The art of living has two aspects: one is to embrace the beauty without clinging so we can let it go freely when it changes and the other is to learn from the difficulties of life how to stop the mind from reinforcing the difficulty by how it reacts to the situation.

Live this life as fully, intensely and 100% focused as possible in the here and now rather than endlessly wondering about what may come later on at the time of death. Actualizing is not necessarily taking on some big mission in life. It is how you do each action in each moment, regardless of what it is. Do all actions with poise and dignity and with total attention on only that. That is all there is to it. It's not what you know, it's how you are. It's not what you've done, it's how you are. Actualizing means being aware and emotionally responsive to others, not just being happy alone. Being emotionally walled off and being lonely are each the cause of the other. Helping others is helping ourselves because we can't be lonely and happy at the same time. Find ways to cultivate the expression of emotional warmth. Sometimes it is as simple as asking "how are you?" with full attention and body language and looking for a small way to be helpful. Give a compliment and thanks for something, focus on the other person a little more. If you give happiness, you get happiness.

Spiritual practice means being aware of how we are keeping our minds in this moment and using that awareness to replace old mental habits that create suffering with new ones that are more helpful. We never eliminate our mental habits but we can replace painful ones with more positive helpful ones. One of the most common negative habits is to constantly remind ourselves of what was wanted and didn't happen while ignoring and not being grateful for the fine things that are present moment to moment.

Insight without compassion creates a cold analytical personality. Compassion without insight makes a good hearted fool. Wisdom requires both insight and compassion working together. Our primary job is to learn what we are and then to manifest that wisdom in the midst of all the jobs of this lifetime. Our personal energy and emotional state both creates and influences the surroundings in unknowable ways. Asking "How can I help?" is a major part of it. We are a social species and there are hard wired mental rewards for strengthening social bonds.

Equanimity comes from being at peace with all of life. Dealing with things as they are in this moment, we can accept that responsibility instead of blaming fate and then we are in control of our lives. We can learn from everything that arises and decide what to do with our lives.

Until we go into the fire of a crisis we cannot know if whatever insight we may think we have is really solid. Welcome the crises as opportunities to move insights from theory to experiential reality. Give something every day, be grateful for something every day, engage with nature every day, even if nature is only a potted plant on a windowsill. That potted plant holds infinity. Right now, in this moment, nothing is lacking.

This slow personality transformation has to be cultivated and practiced for years. Quit too soon and you are not changed. Spiritual practice is like plugging into a source of electricity. Just knowing the outlet is there but not plugging into it doesn't give us the energy that is potentially available. To get the benefit, we have to plug in. We have to keep accessing it all the time with continuous focus and awareness to keep it alive, strong and actively influencing how life is lived rather than just a faint memory. Spiritual practice ought to be an enhancement of life, not a tough grind that you struggle through for the sake of the insights that arise but without any enjoyment of the doing of it. When we not only know but actually live this, the butterfly has finally perched on our outstretched finger. We can only hold out the finger until the butterfly chooses to land. Any attempt to seize a butterfly may well destroy it.

One definition of spirituality is "one's emotional relationship with unanswerable questions." One day the dog came in to the dining room and was frightened by the sudden presence of a green paper bag on the table that had not been there a minute before when she'd left the room. She bristled the fur on her neck, she growled and barked for all she was worth. She meant well, she tried her best to do the right things and guard the territory from this alien intruder, but her mind simply could not grasp and comprehend the situation. Are we like that too? Is trying to comprehend some ultimate meaning or significance to life without making up stories and myths beyond our mental capability, like a chimpanzee wanting to write a symphony? Perhaps not. Experiential insight takes us where rational analysis cannot reach.

Einstein said "The most beautiful and profound emotion we can experience is the sensation of the mystical. It is the source of all true science….To know that what is impenetrable to us really exists, manifesting itself as the highest wisdom and the most radiant beauty … is at the center of true religion."

The great quantum physicist Schrodinger went a step further, asserting that "Inconceivable as it seems to ordinary reason, you – and all other conscious beings as such – are all in all. Hence this life of yours that you are living is not merely a piece of the entire existence, but is in a certain sense the whole. Thus you can throw yourself flat on the ground, stretched out upon Mother Earth, with the certain conviction that you are one with her and she with you."

THE LIGHT IN A SEA GRASS MEADOW

The universe is ultimately beautiful
and mysterious. Directly experiencing
that beauty and mystery with awe and
humility is the essence of being human.

Right now sea turtles are migrating across thousands of miles. Right now sharks on the sea floor are looking for food. Right now a tiger is sleeping under a bush. Right now flowers are attracting insects and making seeds. Our human lives are lived within a space that is vast and ancient and full of all these other beings, which live their lives in the same moment that we live ours. And in this very moment, all of us – tigers, humans, flowers, sharks - are on the surface of a planet hurling through space around a star that is one of billions of stars in a galaxy that is one of billions of galaxies. The universe is ultimately beautiful and mysterious. Directly experiencing that beauty and mystery with awe and humility is the essence of being human.

The next retreat week involved camping at a barrier beach state park instead of at the cypress pond which had to be surrendered to the ticks and mosquitoes until cooler weather returned. The park campground was like a pre-modern village. With no solid walls or air conditioning, and with tiny camping spots all on top of each other, conversation swirled around the place. Incessant speech is the hallmark of humans, yet that is what has to stop to let go of ego. It is impossible without solitude and silence and being in a nonverbal place. While the kids quickly formed bicycle-mounted cavalry units, the adults were more reserved and stayed in their own family units so I still was able to maintain a silent solitary space in the campground.

A flock of shore birds raced up and down the beach. They started in the east, ran and searched for a mile or so to the west then flew back over the water to the starting point and repeated the process. Cormorants sat on some old derelict pilings. Gulls and ospreys dove on fish, and two shrimp boats were anchored offshore. A solitary porpoise hunted fish, moving fast, swimming first one way then the opposite as it surfaced to breathe. Several cormorants and gulls hustled over to sit on the water surface where it was hunting. A big thunderstorm came in off the Gulf of Mexico, making a rainbow overhead. Two or three ospreys hung in the wind hunting, and suddenly a flock of gulls appeared down the beach also hanging motionless on the wind.

The next morning at dawn, two deer stood by the tent window. The September morning was cool and cloudy as I left the campground and hiked about three miles on an old trail through the remote, mostly inaccessible wilderness of the outer end of the barrier spit. A sand pine scrub forest covered the dunes. Unlike the fire-maintained longleaf pine forests further inland, this type of forest is only found on sand dunes, either at the coast or still surviving on inland dunes where ancient shorelines once stood during times of higher sea level. Due to the sterile sand and the speed with which rainwater drains through it, the plants live in a functional desert. Only a few species are present but many of them occur nowhere else. It is a stark landscape of white and dark green, the pines stunted and gnarled by salt spray.

The place was alive with fox squirrels, coyote tracks, five-lined skinks, a chuck wills widow on her nest. After several more miles, the tracks of the endemic endangered beach mice that live nowhere else on earth appeared. I sat for a long time on top of a huge dune watching porpoises working the surf zone hunting fish, Long swells were coming ashore off of a tropical storm that had formed several days before and was slowly wandering our way into the Gulf of Mexico. It was predicted to intensify into the first hurricane of the season.

A hurricane is born, has a name and a history and then dies. Where are the dead hurricanes? What happens to them at their death? At one level of perception, storms, like humans, are unique distinct individuals that are born, exist for a short time, have a unique history and then disappear. But at another level clouds, rain and clear skies are all components of one single thing, the atmosphere, alternating between different states of being – water droplets in the cloud and water vapor in the air. A hurricane, a thunderstorm, a single cloud in a clear sky, they are all different aspects of the same reality. A hurricane is but a momentary configuration in the atmosphere that appears out of the matrix of gases, persists and then disperses back into the atmosphere.

Sunrise and sunset, apparently discrete events, are but a momentary point in the endless spinning of the earth. A river at its source is neither the same nor different from the river halfway downstream or the river as it enters the ocean. All seem to be discretely separate things but are in fact only impermanent configurations within a continuous never ending process. They have no independent reality despite the fact that our senses perceive them as discrete events.

A human lifetime is not so different. We too are born, have a history and then die, but are we also a momentary configuration in an underlying Reality? We spend the hours of our lives surrounded by human things but it's important to touch eternity now and then and the sea is a good place to do it. The birds, the light, the weather are all constantly changing, but the sea is a constant. The shore with houses and families is daily life. Looking the other way to the featureless ocean with no human structures is like facing death, a vast unknown with no property, no family names and no human social activities. Beyond the blank sea surface, however, is a wondrous world of endless sentient beings. The sea is the closest thing to eternity that we can see and touch directly.

As I hiked and sat in the sand pine scrub, the huge white dunes and along the bayside of the peninsula, there was no being restless, just endless walking. Walking, walking, walking. By midday, the temperature was at least 98 degrees with no shade or fresh water anywhere and I was soon soaked in sweat. Heat and thirst silenced the last mental chatter. As the chattering mind faded into silence, it once again became more and more clear that I was simply a momentary aspect of that creation and in no way separate from it. Here and now just perceive clearly, see clearly, hear clearly without words. Stop talking, stop thinking, there is nothing you won't understand, said an old master.

The underlying energy of the universe was manifest as storm clouds constantly forming, changing, dissolving, reforming and sweeping overhead. Reality is always and constantly shape-shifting, dissolving its old appearances and manifesting new ones but all these appearances are only the patterns on the surface.

I accidently flushed a nesting diamondback terrapin on the bay side beach. She raced into the sea grass covered tide flat that was almost dry at low tide and then stopped, apparently too exhausted to keep wading through the shallows. I apologized for disturbing her but she stared at me in reptilian silence. Another half circle of rainbow formed around the sun.

That evening, I kayaked into the sea grass meadow and sat in waist-deep warm shallow water with a full moon in the eastern blue sky. To the north the sky was purple and gold with a huge thunderhead slowly building from east to west across the sky toward the sun which was low in a clear blue sky. The palm trees lining the bay shore glowed in the intense colors of the day as three schools of porpoises hunted mullet in the bay. The big fish jumped everywhere and the sea grass and sand bars were full of sand dollars and other small animals. The moment hummed with awareness. If spiritual practice doesn't give happiness, it is not being done right.

I reached for a pencil, but it wasn't there, having floated through the meshes of the bag. The underwater Plexiglas slate was useless. The grass bed was full of live pen shells, big triangular-shaped clams that sat upright, the spiny upper edge of the shell several inches above the surface of the sand. Normally uncommon, this year these relatives of the scallops were everywhere. The shells gaped widely, exposing the orange and brown curtain of soft tissue between the shells to the bright sunlight. Inside the tissue were microscopic single- celled plants that the clam cultivates like a garden, providing a secure space and its own wastes as fertilizer. The plant cells provide extra food to the clam, supplementing what it filters out of the seawater.

A father toadfish guarded its eggs inside an empty pen shell. All mouth and teeth and ready to use them, toadfish give a new meaning to the word ugly, but at night they sing to each other, an elegant eerie song in the darkness. Clumps of mussels, smaller surface-living bivalves, were scattered about like islands in the grass. Blennies, little brown fish an inch long, hid in empty mussel shells that were mixed in with the live ones.

Except for the grass, it looked vaguely like a reconstruction of an ancient seafloor of millions of years ago, in the days before strong jawed fish and crabs with their powerful crushing claws appeared and drove most surface-living shelled animals to extinction. Snail species with easily crushed open spiral shells became extinct and were replaced with species possessing stronger, spinier, crush-resistant shells. Giant oysters, which once reached several feet in length and dominated the reefs, disappeared. Modern oysters are now largely restricted to estuarine areas where low salinity protects them.

When it got dark, I pitched a tent on a nearby dock. Walking out on the dock, each footstep glowed with blue fire on wet spots where somebody's cast net had landed earlier and left a wet spot on the wooden boards. The thin film of water was full of microscopic bioluminescent plankton. These blue fire footsteps in the dark were both the magic of life and also the impermanence of life and death. All those glowing microorganisms would soon be dead. The beauty of steps of fire or the manifestation of life and death, they were both at once, there was no either/or in it, and no blue fire appeared until the human walked there.

The tide was just below the top of an oyster bar. Comb jellies hit the shells in blazing balls of electric blue green fire on the dark water surface. When the tide rose above the bar, the show was over and gone as if it never happened. A breeze created a rhythmic sound of small waves. A pattering from the wavelets hitting marsh grass along the shore provided the chords. The pattern of black dock shadow on the steely grey black face of the water constantly flowed and moved on the surface of the water.

A sky full of moonlight and glowing white clouds created an ever-moving canvas of black, white and pearl that yielded an ever more splendid unfolding. The breeze died and the bay below the clouds developed a mirror finish that reflected each white cloud on the black-and-silver polished surface. A scattering of dusty stars gleamed in between puffy huge pearly mounds of clouds. As the moon sank in the west, the pearly clouds turned to grey but the stars become brighter and brighter, stars swaying on the flat calm surface of the water below the dock, stars glittering overhead when I lay on a bench staring upward, stars hanging in the branches of the black pines silhouetted behind the dunes. Lying in the dark, my consciousness became an infinite flowing through time and space, not separate and distinct from the stars and the sea. All the accomplishments of the ego-self would soon dissolve, fade and be forgotten as had any possible previous lives or even last night's dream, but time spent in such a place gave something more permanent. The traditional 5 hindrances to Zen practice – longing for the world, ill will and anger, sleepiness, restlessness and doubt – had all disappeared. Total freedom practice had appeared with no struggle, so great joy arose in each moment whether it was a moment of meditation or a moment of activity. Having sat and struggled for many years at formal retreats in the temple pressure cooker with a painful body and the frenetic mind of dissatisfaction, burning off the personal hindrances that had kept me tied up in knots, now I felt like I was finally doing this practice correctly. And it had all come together without any special effort.

By 4 AM, the moon had set and the world was dark and starry with stars above and stars below swaying on the black sea's surface. The air was full of the sounds of multiple porpoises hunting in the dark starry sea, huffing and tail slapping. An alligator underneath the dock exploded into a tail slapping dive as I walked across the boards above it. At dawn, four porpoises passed in a flat calm bay in front of the dock just as a red sun rose over the marsh and a bay that was blue and red. Poof, poof, silence, poof! A sudden white spray of water shot up across the bay as the porpoises made a strike.

As the morning sun rose higher, swirls of gold fire exploded everywhere as schools of small fish broke the surface and bigger fish struck them. For a long time, I had felt that sun glitter on water had some information within it that I could not decipher. That morning I finally knew how to read it. Glitter fills the mind until insight translates the message into human awareness. What I was seeking is present day or night, hot or cold, raining or sunny – we all are always carrying the potential for that to happen at any time. Sometimes we can capture it in words and sometimes there are no words in the experience.

Against the expanse of sun glitter on the bay the black silhouette of another dock shimmered as did the black silhouette of a snowy egret when it landed on the dock railing. In that golden and black haze, all of life and all that had ever happened for an entire lifetime came together into one sharp focus in that moment. That precise moment was an always-present absolute perfection. Tide rises, breathing in, tide falls, breathing out. Although I had often failed to be aware of it, that perfection had never once failed to be present.

The following titles provide an intro-
duction to investigations of non-local mental phenomena. Some authors
view consciousness within a materialistic framework while others present evidence for non-brain based forms of consciousness. It is only a
starting point. Each reader must determine for themselves what is credible and what is not.

Andresen, J. and R.K.C. Forman. 2000. Cognitive Models and Spiritual Maps. Imprint Academic, Bowling Green, Ky. 287 pp.

Austin, J.H. 1999. Zen and the Brain: Toward an Understanding of
Meditation and Consciousness. MIT Press. Cambridge, Ma. 844 pp.

Austin, J.H. 2009. Selfless Insight: Zen and the Meditative
Transformation of Consciousness. MIT Press. 352 pp.

Bownds, M.D. 1999. The Biology of Mind: Origins and Structures
of Mind, Brain, and Consciousness. Fitzgerald Science Press, Bethesda,
Md. 357 pp.

Broderick, D. 2007. Outside the Gates of Science: Why it's time for
the paranormal to come in from the cold. Running Press.

Cardena, E. (ed.), S.J. Lynn (ed), S. C. Krippner(ed.). 2004.
Varieties of Anomalous Experience: Examining the Scientific Evidence.
American Psychological Association. 476 pp.

Carter. C. 2007. Parapsychology and the Skeptics: A scientific argument for the existence of esp. Sterling House Books

Carter, C. 2010. Science and the Near Death Experience: How Consciousness Survives death. Inner traditions. 320 pp.

Chalmers, D. J. 1996. The Conscious Mind: In Search of a Fundamental Theory. Oxford University Press. New York. 414 pp.

Chalmers, D. 2010. The Character of Consciousness. Oxford University Press, USA.

D'Aquili, E. and A.B. Newberg. 1999. The Mystical Mind: Probing the Biology of Religious Experience. Fortress Press, Minneapolis, Mn. 228 pp.

Edelman, G. and G. Tononi. 2000. A Universe of Consciousness: How Matter Becomes Imagination. Basic Books. New York. 274 pp.

Frohock, F.M. 2000. Lives of the Psychics: The Shared Worlds of Science and Mysticism. University of Chicago Press, Chicago. 281 pp.

Goswami, A. 1993. The Self Aware Universe: How Consciousness Creates the Material World. Penguin Putnam. New York. 319 pp.

Kaufman, Stuart. 1995. At Home in the Universe: The Search for the Laws of Self Organization and Complexity. Oxford University Press, New York. 321.

Kaufman, Stuart. 2008. Reinventing the Sacred: A New View of Science, Reason and Religion. Basic Books, New York. 320 pp.

Parnia, S. 2006. What Happens When We Die: A Groundbreaking Study Into the Nature of Life and Death. Hay House, London. 200 pp.

Kelly, et. Al. 2002. Irreducible Mind. Toward a Psychology for the 21st century. Rowman and Littlefield Publishersw, New York.

Radin, D. 1997. The Conscious Universe: The Scientific Truth of Psychic Phenomena. Harper Edge, San Francisco.362 pp.

Sabom, M. 1982. Recollections of Death: A Medical Investigation. Simon and Schuster, New York. 224 pp.

Shroder, T. 1999. Old Souls: The Scientific Evidence for Past Lives. Simon and Schuster. 253 pp.

Stevenson, I. 1974. 20 Cases Suggestive of Reincarnation. University Press of Virginia, Charlottesville. 396 pp.

Stevenson, I. 1992. Children Who Remember Past Lives: A Question of Reincarnation. University Press of Virginia, Charlottesville. 354 pp.

Targ, R. and J. Katra. 1999. Miracles of Mind: Exploring Non Local Consciousness and Spiritual Healing. New World Library, Novato, Ca. 333 pp.

Tart, C. 2009. The End of Materialism: How evidence of the paranormal is bringing science and spirit together. New Harbinger Publicaions

Taylor, J. B. 2006. My Stroke of Insight: A Brain Scientist's Personal Journey. Viking Press. New York. 183 pp.

ABOUT THE AUTHOR

Anne Rudloe lives in Panacea, Florida. She and her husband run the Gulf Specimen Marine Laboratory, an independent nonprofit environmental center and aquarium. She received her Ph.D. from Florida State University, where she has taught courses and done research in marine biology and environmental issues. Her writing has appeared in *National Geographic, Smithsonian Magazine*, and scientific journals. She is the author of *Butterflies on a Sea Wind: Beginning Zen.* She is a co-author of *Shrimp: The Endless Quest for Pink Gold* and *Priceless Florida: Natural Ecosystems and Native Species.* She received Inka or permission to teach Zen in 2011 from the Kwan Um School of Zen.

95214403R00095

Made in the USA
Columbia, SC
07 May 2018